Expan

"Widowhood can be d
ance from women who have walked the same path in their own life's
journey. Insight into to the numbness, despair, trauma, and the path back
to survival and resiliency is provided through their words. With all the
guidance that there may be in the world, there's something powerful and
moving about the stories of the weary yet determined feet that survived
walking the journey of one of the worst times in their lives."
—Dr. Rosalyn Y. Brown Beatty, LPC, NCC – Mental Health
Clinician and Trauma & Grief Expert

"In my initial conversations with Arlene Sacks, I believed this work would
be informative and helpful, yet also entertaining. I recognized immediately that a project such as this would be important and make a wonderful
book, especially because most of us enjoy reading. We will all ultimately
be by ourselves, regardless of loving families, so this is a necessary project
that will impact women as they progress through the stages of their lives,
planned and unplanned. It was my pleasure and honor to contribute to
this book."
—Mary

"Losing a spouse, no matter how it happens, is a most difficult time.
Everything seems overwhelming. Reading about other women's experiences and how they dealt with their challenges always helps. If we give
them hope through our stories, they will get through this. Sharing these
stories with Arlene, a storyteller herself, provides support for each woman
to grieve in her own unique way."
—Lorraine

"I experienced the tragedy of widowhood twice, at two very different ages.
Each time, I sought and was given help by psychologists, social workers,
and hospice groups. However, the very best explanations, guidance, and
support came from other widows. Arlene Sacks has given me the opportunity and guidance to help other widows through sharing our stories."
—Barbara

"I believe this book of shared stories reminds us we are not alone and
that together, we can move forward. This book reminds us that we gain
strength by sharing our individual processes, and, as Arlene explains, even
if we don't realize we have them."
—Sallie

MOVING FORWARD

MOVING FORWARD

The Widow's Journey

ARLENE SACKS

Redwood Publishing, LLC

Published by Redwood Publishing, LLC
Orange County, California
www.redwooddigitalpublishing.com

ISBN 978-1-956470-23-9 (hardcover)
ISBN 978-1-956470-17-8 (paperback)
ISBN 978-1-956470-18-5 (e-book)

Library of Congress Control Number: 2021920385

Cover Design by Redwood Publishing
Book Design and Production by Jose Pepito
Editing by Avery Auer

To Mara,
I know, you know, and now he knows.

ONCE UPON A TIME, a couple returned from their tenth trip to Scandinavia (don't ask) and went to the doctor for their annual checkups. This was always uneventful, as nothing was ever wrong with them. They took no medications and were happy and healthy. Until that day. On that day, their world and a relationship of over half a century began to come crashing down around them.

CONTENTS

A JOURNEY OF GROWTH

"We tell ourselves stories in order to live."

—Joan Didion

The writing of this book has been an experience in moving beyond my thoughts about my relationship with my husband to contemplating life as a widow, which includes my relationships with many others. In the process, I have discovered that love stories, like mine (as well as inanimate objects, such as this book) can actually develop lives of their own. As affection, intimacy, and passion develop, the story of every couple changes. Real life abruptly moves in, and the stories of others intersect with one's own—which is why this book has ended up transcending the story of Howard and Arlene. It has become a compilation of stories about being a couple . . . and then not being one, and about life, values, and home. It is life's love story as it has been shared by many.

Over the years, I came to recognize that someday I might lose my husband, and that it would be a catastrophic loss. What I never expected was that, along with the horrific pain, I would also lose a huge piece of my identity and my life as I knew it. I had no way of understanding that when you lose a spouse, you must learn to move forward and function, even as your entire soul is being ripped to pieces. When that fact hit me, I feared I wouldn't be strong enough to do it—to keep it together and continue living.

The best way I can describe the process of moving forward after losing someone so close to you is by comparing the process to a train ride. When you envision a train, you can picture a long line of separate compartments. Life moves forward from the last compartment to the first. As you progress in life, you slowly move from one car to the next, eventually shutting the door to the previous compartment and becoming content in the next one . . . until it's time to move forward again. That moving forward, letting go of one door and stretching for the next one, often shakes every part of you, but sometimes it may feel as if you've moved from one compartment to another without even having been aware of the moment it occurred. Mostly, you are trembling across the unknown. When I lost the love of my life, I was keenly aware of every single movement, often as if it were in slow motion. I chose to open the door and reach for the next compartment, still seeing the compartments behind me but moving forward to the next one on my own. I find comfort in knowing I can always look back to see and remember everything inside of them, while I also know there is so much more to do in the one I'm in now.

This book is, first and foremost, the story of my life with Howard from age seventeen through sixty-six. It began with the kind of chemistry that hits like a bolt of lightning. There is actually an Italian phrase for this, *colpo di fulmine*, implying a thunderbolt so powerful and intense that it cannot be denied. Love may strike this way, at first glance, or it may develop quietly over time, from friendship through that first kiss to a quiet mutual recognition—but however it comes, there is no going back. Chemistry wins. For us, that chemistry took hold quickly and never let go for over fifty years.

I like to describe our life together as a kind of dance. Sometimes we waltzed and twirled effortlessly, sometimes we engaged in a tango, and sometimes we stepped on each other's toes. But we were always touching and taking turns leading. Since Howard's death, I have had to learn how to dance alone, to move forward with a partner I can't see or feel. I circle the room as the music continues to play and the room continues to spin, knowing I must somehow keep dancing.

I wrote this book to share my process of moving forward— continuing to dance—without Howard. My purpose is to help other widows while keeping my husband's memory alive. When I began writing, I believed I was sharing a process that had begun at the moment of my widowhood. What I have discovered is that the process actually began before Howard died—some nine months earlier, when he began to share with me the things he wanted me to do to prepare myself for his death.

While he was trying to prepare me, I was trying hard to get my three parts—head, heart, and body—to act in sync with the reality before us. None of those three aspects of my being ever really believed Howard would die. They *knew* it; they understood the disease and its implications, but they never actually *believed* it.

Up until that nine-month mark, Howard and I had still been intimate. We'd still been able to enjoy a quick stop at a café, a short dinner out, a visit with friends. As the doctor managing his care was located in California, we would fly from Florida to see him. However, in February of 2013, Howard could no longer tolerate the physical stress of airplane travel. Thus, I found myself having to take him by ship. On that trip, everything changed, as each day, his physical condition deteriorated. To be clear, I *still* did not believe he was dying. My head was still enjoying our conversations, my heart was still dancing, and my body was still his. But it was at that point that the process of my widowhood began.

Howard *did* believe that he was dying and felt he had to address it by doing what he could to help my transition. He cared so much that he used his time and remaining strength to share with me instructions on how to handle those things for which he had always been responsible. He understood that it was time for me to begin shifting into another role.

In addition to its mission of helping other widows, this book is a love story devoted to honoring a relationship, a marriage, and its inevitable end.

In the process of writing it—and quite by surprise, at first—I was joined by thirteen other widows eager to share their stories with me. (They came to me one by one, as a result of a few thoughtful people in whom I confided and who, in turn, sent others my way.) Ultimately, the journeys of these women supplemented and augmented my own, providing examples of the multiple paths widows take on their way forward.

I like to think that I did not choose these stories, but that they chose me. The fact that these women turned out to be a diverse group with sharply differing experiences and perspectives was as unexpected as everything else about my process. They come from different cultures (Christian, Jewish, Black, Asian, Hispanic, European) and different countries (USA, Japan, Portugal/France, Cuba, India, Jamaica). They are of various ages (from thirty-four to eighty-two) and sexual orientations. Their spouses died from illnesses and accidents. Some of them had adult children at the moment their widowhood began; some, teenagers; some, infants; and some, no children at all. One had been widowed previously.

I hope that by sharing their experiences along with my own, I have presented a variety of role models for other women and that the story of each woman in this book will be relatable to a particular reader who needs to hear it. As a group, we are diverse, yet we share a bond. We have all gone through the process of moving forward after being widowed, and we have all talked about that process frankly here. These women have become my heroes, and I am eternally grateful that they were willing to share their stories with me—and ultimately, with you.

My love story, my bereavement, and my evolution into the person I am now are bound up in the creation of this book. Likewise, the experiences of my friends, my family members, and the other widows I interviewed are part of it as well. In the end, the book has taken on a life of its own—as more than the sum of its parts—and the thoughts and feelings captured in it guide my progress every day.

MY SISTER WIDOWS

Sallie

Sallie had been married for forty-six years when her husband died in 2013, within thirty-three days of diagnosis of a fast-moving cancer. Ted had been disabled two years into their marriage, when he lost three limbs in Vietnam, so Sallie had been taking care of him since 1970. She had become accomplished in carrying out many tasks women aren't always asked to do, but Ted was able to work in finance, handle the bills, and master investing.

Kelly

Kelly was married twice. Her first marriage lasted about a decade and ended in divorce. After sixteen years, during which she became self-sufficient, she remarried. George came to the marriage with three children, whom Kelly felt better prepared to handle after her years on her own. After twenty-five years, George became seriously ill, and they endured a horrific three years leading up to his death in 2015.

Netti

Netti had been married to Wilbur for twenty-two years, and he had just turned sixty when he died in 2016—fifteen months after his diagnosis of stage II cancer in several organs. Netti had previously been married for around eight years and divorced for fourteen. She worked for the Urban League and had just given three months' notice when Wilbur came home from work one day, experiencing shortness of breath. The next day, they received his diagnosis.

Mary

Takako, known as Mary, was born in Japan and became a nurse. She moved to the United States as a young woman. She was eighty-one and living in Northern California when we first spoke, having been a widow for nineteen years. She and her late husband, Bruce, had met in the States and moved to Gothenburg, Sweden, where they had their first of five children before moving back to the US. Six years before Bruce died, he developed dementia, requiring Mary to make many difficult decisions.

Sara

Sara was born in Portugal, moved to the US, and finally settled in France. She currently lives on a farm outside Paris. In 1986, at the age of thirty-four, she was widowed quite unexpectedly when her husband, Michel, died in an accident. At that time, she had two young children—a girl and a boy, aged seven and eight. She stayed home for about six months to care for them after the tragedy, at which point her need to move forward began.

Lorraine

Lorraine is a fairly well-known artist in South Florida. Her husband, John, a pilot, died in a small-plane crash in 2000—about fifteen years before we spoke. As she described the experience, he went off to work one day and never came home. She had two adult children at the time. One of them was preparing to get married when her husband died, and as Lorraine planned the wedding, she found herself planning a funeral as well.

Paulina

Paulina was married to Teri for twenty-one years before she lost her to a prolonged illness. Their love affair had begun as a friendship, and they always remained "best friends." They were confident that they would enjoy a long life and grow old together, so Teri's death in 2018, at age sixty, came as a terrible shock in spite of the painful process that led up to it.

Rosalyn

Unlike the other widows I spoke with, Rosalyn was someone I knew personally. She was very young when she became a widow, just thirty-five, with children aged three and seven. Her husband, Ril, had been just thirty-six, but had suffered from liver and kidney disease for seven years. By the time I interviewed Rosalyn specifically for this book, she had been widowed for three years. As a counselor, she knew the impact of trauma on young children, so her process of moving forward was quite purposeful, with her kids always in mind.

Donna

Donna had been married and divorced when she met Ray, to whom she remained married for over twenty-five years and with whom she had two sons. In 2008, when Ray died of complications of dementia at age seventy-three, he was living in a convalescent home. Before she moved him there for his safety, Donna would periodically find him on the deck of their house in the middle of the night, a most dangerous place to be, as they lived on the side of a hill. Now in her eighties, she is dealing with decisions that are extraordinarily stressful.

Margaret

Margaret was married for thirty-three years when her husband, Mike, died of lung cancer. Within the five years following his death, she lost her mother, her sister, and her father. With her support system decimated, it was difficult and painful for her to keep moving forward—but she was kind enough to speak to me about the process. Margaret is one of only two widows who moved out of her marital home in the aftermath of her spouse's death.

Barbara
A scientist as well as a prolific artist, Barbara is the only member of my "sisterhood" to have been widowed twice. Her first husband died along with her son in an airplane crash over twenty years ago, when she was forty-seven. After several years passed, she remarried a man named Butch, an architect. Twenty years later, in 2018, he died. She brings a unique perspective to this book for several reasons, not the least of which is that she also lost a child. I was grateful to speak with someone who could share the differences of widowhood at various stages of life.

Anusuya
Anusuya (Anu) is from India and had been a widow over four years when we first spoke. Her husband, Gautam, died at the age of fifty-eight after a battle with Huntington's disease, which is transmitted genetically and for which there is no cure. Gautam died suddenly of an embolism just five days before their son's wedding. Since then, both Anu's mother and mother-in-law have also passed away. Her process of moving forward has been affected by particular aspects of her culture that she was kind enough to discuss with me.

Sharon
In 1999, Sharon's husband, Dennis—twenty-five years her senior—was diagnosed with advanced prostate cancer that had already metastasized. They lived in Jamaica, where both of them were born, and she was told that the hospitals there were not equipped to treat him. They were advised to go to Miami, which they did in 2000. Dennis was a scientist, and they both understood

the implications of his diagnosis. Their children, a boy and a girl, aged seven and six at the time they moved, went to stay with relatives in New York. After Dennis died, Sharon and the kids settled in Miami, where they still live.

PART I

A BICYCLE BUILT FOR TWO BECOMES A UNICYCLE

TO CHARACTERIZE MARRIAGE AS a bicycle built for two may seem obvious. So might the idea of widowhood as a unicycle, which is much trickier and more perilous to master. What is not obvious is what it takes to get off that tandem bike and onto that hard-to-handle one-wheeler. Some women find they have a knack for it, regaining their balance with relative ease. Others fall repeatedly and have to apply discipline to get back up and try again. The process of learning to balance and ride off alone epitomizes the transition into widowhood—what I call *Moving Forward*. Understanding this is one thing; experiencing it is quite another.

CHAPTER ONE

MOVING INTO WIDOWHOOD

"I am not afraid of storms, for I am learning to sail my ship."

—Louisa May Alcott

During the third year after Howard's death, something unexpected happened. Three women, independently of one another and from different areas of my life, suggested I write about my experiences—my "process," as they put it. I hadn't really considered that I had a process, but they seemed to believe I did. They suggested other women might be interested in the organized, disciplined process I had created for myself.

Frankly, this bewildered me. After all, I was just "doing what had to be done."

Each of these women who knew me well and had met my husband many times explained that I had created a process. I can see that now, although I hadn't thought of it that way. Over the course of three years, I had learned about and taken care of home repairs, figured out all of the paperwork that was now my responsibility, and made financial and business decisions. Additionally, I had organized the upstairs level of my house, including such tasks as scanning thousands of photos and disposing of furniture I no longer needed. And I'd done it all one step at a time.

Were these women justified in their belief that I should write a book to help others in my situation? Perhaps they didn't realize that, although I had worked in responsible jobs for over fifty years, I'd been petrified of many mundane things that Howard had always taken care of. It might be hard to believe, but before he got sick, I had never put gas in my car; gone to a car wash; called a plumber, an electrician, or a pool person; dealt with our financial life beyond earning a paycheck; shopped for insurance; spoken with an attorney or accountant; titled the cars; or even made travel arrangements. How was I qualified to tell others how to live their lives?

At the end of Year Four, I shared with my hairdresser the conversations I'd had with the three women. After listening to me for a few minutes, he put down his scissors, looked me in the eye, and said, "Arlene, they are absolutely right. As a matter of fact, I have two clients who are widows, married twenty-five and forty-seven years respectively. And, although they haven't followed your process exactly, they've both stayed in their homes, learned to fix them up and live in them independently, and moved forward with their lives. I have other clients who haven't done anything like that. Maybe you and these two widows need to get together and talk."

What ultimately developed from his suggestion were conversations with thirteen other widows, each with their own processes of moving forward.

The final thing that got me going was a heated conversation with a male friend. When I explained to him my aversion to the statement people often made that I needed to "move on," he suggested I might think of it in slightly different terms. Maybe they didn't exactly mean *move on*, but rather, *move forward*.

I saw what he meant right away. To me, *moving on* implied that I'd be leaving Howard behind rather than keeping him with me. That just wasn't something I could do. After approximately fifty years with him, I had no intention of moving on from Howard. How could I? But the idea of *moving forward* switched on a light bulb in my head and produced a chill throughout my entire body. I knew how to move forward; I had been doing it my whole life.

By opening this new door, my friend set me on a new path. Those two words—*move forward*—provided the perspective I needed. I knew that step by step, year by year, I could move forward. It didn't mean I would have to move on!

It would take me another year to begin to write, making it a full five years since my circumstances had changed so radically.

"WRITE IT DOWN!"

"Our dead are never dead to us until we have forgotten them."
—George Eliot

In January 2014, three months after Howard died, I had to travel to Cincinnati for teaching work. When I got there, the university president, Roger Sublett, called and asked if I was up to joining him and his wife, Cindy, for brunch, as Howard and I had done many times over the years. We'd enjoyed a lovely relationship with this couple, and I gratefully accepted the invitation.

We arrived at the same time and were shown to a table surrounded by four chairs. After an awkward moment during which the three of us stared at that fourth chair, Roger asked, "Do you think Howard would mind if we put our coats on his chair?" The tension broke instantly, and I smiled, pleased that he was acknowledging Howard's presence. I assured him it would be fine, and we all took our seats for a nice visit.

As we reminisced about the meals the four of us had shared over twelve years, I found myself talking about the many extraordinary things Howard had done during his last nine months. Although he could no longer walk, he'd been intent on making my future life without him easier.

"Write these things down," urged Roger, "so you don't forget any of them as time goes by."

When I got home from that trip to Cincinnati, I finally took his advice and wrote down each specific thing Howard had done or instructed me to do. When I'd completed the list, I placed it at the top of my desk, never dreaming it would become the skeleton of a book I'd develop. But that's where the book you are now reading began.

HOWARD'S LAST NINE MONTHS

"The one of us who finds the strength to get up first, must help the other."
—Vera Nazarian

In February 2013, after Howard's bones gave way and caused him to collapse, robbing him of his mobility, he understood that he should begin teaching me as well as preparing me to live without him. When I protested, he explained that our time was short and that was that. We had much to do if he were going to help me continue to live my life safely and sanely.

He was both teaching me and trying to take care of me—participating in the transition to my taking care of myself. It was as though both of us had been peddling that bicycle built for two, working together yet handling different aspects of our lives in synchronicity. After the diagnosis, we both realized that the tandem bike was going away, and it would be just me on a unicycle. I recognized that I needed some help in learning to ride that unicycle, and I was terrified. It was the last thing I'd ever envisioned or wanted. But Howard stayed with me, holding on as I began to feel safe. Teaching me certain things and facilitating my transition to my new life brought him—and me—greater peace of mind.

What I didn't realize at the time, but have figured out during the development of this book, is that this constituted my first step forward. Howard was still with me, guiding and teaching me, but I was entering the first phase of my own process. The items that follow are all things he felt were important to impart before leaving my side.

THINGS HOWARD TRIED TO TEACH ME

The Stock Market

In February 2013, eight months before Howard died, we made plans to go on a cruise to Los Angeles to consult a specialist. Flying would have been faster—the cruise would take two weeks—but Howard was no longer able to fly.

After boarding the ship, as we approached our stateroom, Howard collapsed. From that point on, he was unable to walk normally. Our life was changing; he would need constant assistance. But our immediate goal was to get to that California doctor who, we prayed, would give us more time together. Thankfully, he did just that, but our physical life had become more complicated.

Back home, Howard was insistent that he and I spend between fifteen and twenty minutes each day discussing the stock market. I had never had a modicum of interest in the subject, and I didn't understand any of the jargon. Undeterred, Howard told me quite firmly that I had better learn about the market and that even if I were to never make a penny, I'd have to learn how to avoid losing one. I nodded and acquiesced, but I'm pretty sure I looked like a deer in the headlights.

From that day forward, like a rat in a maze, I practiced accessing our stock and retirement accounts; checking them; watching specific stocks; and learning when, how, and what to sell. Knowing how to get out was my safety net, Howard explained. His philosophy was to avoid investing in companies that cater to what people *want*, in favor of companies that provide what people *need*. I was to keep his advice in mind no matter what I heard from others.

Patiently, he taught me how to enter everything on graph paper, regardless of the fact that computer records might be easier and more accurate. He believed I would eventually get a "feel" for investing (which never actually happened) and that I would learn to use the money we had freely enough that I could enjoy my life. I can't say that happened either, although I have dipped into our savings on occasion.

Eight months from the time of our lessons about money—after Howard had died—I found myself diligently looking after our investments on a daily basis. While I didn't care if I made a single cent, just as he'd instructed, I tried hard not to lose one. He'd been a wonderful provider who had worked, saved, and invested for my benefit. My goal was to live up to that example.

Taxes and Insurance

Howard had the oddest way of preparing for our annual property tax and homeowners insurance payments. Every month, he would send $1,600 by check to a small local bank—not the one where we kept most of our accounts. I couldn't imagine why he'd do such a thing. He explained that, because the account was earmarked strictly for covering these large annual payments, the money would always be there when it was needed. I was skeptical, but he asked me to try it for six months following his death, and if I found it to be too much trouble, I could then do what I wanted. So be it.

I handled the money his way for a few months and found that, as usual, he was 100 percent right. When the first tax and insurance bills were due, I wrote checks from the small account with no worries about what was in the main account. To this day, I have continued making monthly deposits of $1,600 and have never had to give a moment's thought to how I'd cover these expenses.

Howie had an economic rationale for everything he did, but the main lesson for me was that a simple plan can turn a big challenge into no challenge at all. In this regard and many others, Howie was a great man and teacher.

THINGS HOWARD DID TO TAKE CARE OF ME

Eyeglasses

As an orthodontist, Howie occasionally had a patient who could get him a good price on something. One of them supplied optometrists with eyeglass frames and lenses, and he got us a good discount, which was beneficial for our quickly aging eyes.

When Howard knew his death was imminent, he told me to take his glasses and sunglasses to our ophthalmologist and have my lenses put into his frames.

"Don't be silly," I said. "I can do that . . . later on."

"Absolutely not," he responded, quite agitated. "Take care of it right now!"

What could I do but fetch the glasses and go?

When I'd accomplished this task, Howard was happy (or as happy as he could be). He'd had no intention of allowing me to miss out on a good discount.

Airline Mileage

About a month before he died, Howie asked me to call American Airlines and have them transfer his frequent-flyer miles to me. He was so sick at the time that I suggested this, too, was something that could wait.

Again, he said, "I want you to take care of it now."

So I called American Airlines right in front of him and explained the situation. Much to my surprise, the agent explained that there was a standard form for this (unbelievable!), but it couldn't be submitted until "afterward."

While still on the phone, I quickly shared this with Howard, who remained adamant that the transfer be made immediately.

Overhearing our exchange, the agent said, "Madam, I understand your situation. Why don't I email you the form now, so you'll have it to fill out later?"

His kindness—which I will never forget—satisfied my dying husband. The miles were easily transferred in due time, and someday I will enjoy using them.

A Visit to a Favorite Store

When Howard could no longer walk, we hired an assistant named Benjamin to help him with his bathing and other personal needs. Benjamin ended up spending most of the day on his computer, but when we needed him, he was essential.

About six weeks before Howard died, while I was at work, Howard made arrangements for Benjamin to accompany the two of us to one of my favorite stores, which was approximately forty-five minutes away. We had agreed on the importance of my continuing to work, and Howard wanted me to keep up the professional image I had established—to continue "dressing for success." His plan was that we would go to this store the following

Tuesday and buy a few work outfits for me—and he didn't want to hear that I had plenty of clothes already.

Prior to our trip, I called and asked to speak to a store manager. A lovely gentleman named Dana Stoloff answered, and I explained the nature of our impending visit.

I knew that the car ride would be terribly exhausting for Howard, but when we arrived, we were met by Dana. He and Benjamin spent time with Howard—who was confined to a wheelchair—chatting and reading the newspaper while I shopped. When I'd completed my purchases, Dana, clearly touched by our situation, treated us to lunch at a casual restaurant several doors down from the shop.

By the time we got home, Howard was terribly uncomfortable. He ended up sleeping through the entire next day, but when he woke up, he made me model the clothes I'd bought and was delighted by the result.

A Visit to My Other Favorite Store

Two weeks later, in spite of the toll our first expedition had taken on him, Howard insisted we take a trip to yet another store I love—also around forty-five minutes away. This store is frequented by the rich and famous, and there was almost nothing I felt we could afford there, save, perhaps, a scarf. I had purchased a few small items over the years, and had saved for five years to buy our daughter a special bag there for her thirtieth birthday, to complete her image as the consummate attorney.

Howard told me he wanted to make one last purchase: a final addition to my professional wardrobe. On the appointed day, we parked illegally, directly outside the entrance, and Benjamin carried him in. Lovingly, my husband told me to buy something beautiful for work so that he'd know I'd always look my professional best.

Uppermost in my thoughts was getting Howard safely back home—but there, right in front of us, was a beautiful long red silk scarf. He loved it, and so did I. We purchased it and were out of the store in fifteen minutes.

On the ride home, Howard's medication began to wear off. His occasional gasps were the only sound in the car, and the moment we got back, he went to lie down. We didn't know it, but it would be the last time he'd leave that bed.

The Cars

A couple of weeks before he died, Howard asked me to call both of our children. He wanted to tell each one to purchase a brand-new, safe, family-friendly car that would suit the lives they were leading in Florida. He hoped that each time they drove those vehicles, they would think of him. This was not an expression of ego or a need for appreciation. He knew that those cars would serve as a refuge where, after they'd dropped his grandchildren off at school or some activity, they could sit alone, smile, and think about their dad.

He elicited a promise from each of them that they would select the make and model they wanted, and instructed me to write each one a check and see to it that the money was used as intended. He made them promise to buy the cars before the end of the year.

Our son has since told me that each time he gets into his car to head off to his graduate school classes, he smiles, feels good about himself, and says, "Thank you, Dad." Our daughter reports going through a similar ritual. Anyone who knew Howard knows that he would never spoil his children but would always provide what he believed they needed. That practice continued to the end of his life and beyond.

You've just read numerous examples of what made Howard a great man. Why did I feel the need to share all this with readers who have their own precious memories to revisit? Upon reflection, I believe it is because I have come to think about Howard beyond his role as my life partner. Perhaps you will find yourself doing the same about your departed loved one. In his absence, I have come to appreciate Howard for the man he was as well as the husband he was throughout our fifty-year relationship.

From the time Howard was seventeen until he was about thirty, his focus was on the study of science and how he could develop his professional skills and abilities. During that same period, he married me, we created a family, and we moved among four states. He discovered the joys of Broadway musicals, serious plays, and museums. He was growing into the man he would become, adding pieces that would be integral to his life until the day he died.

It was in his thirties that Howard extended his interests into the areas of home construction and maintenance. Shortly after his fortieth birthday, he began to acquire knowledge about the business of finance and investing. From the age of forty until his death at sixty-six, he worked to bring together the various pieces of his life and work. As in a jigsaw puzzle, each piece was significant, and ultimately they formed a beautiful picture of Howard, the man.

I now understand all of the ways and reasons why Howard was a great man. He came to believe that there were no limits to a person's potential. He never focused on what he could not do, but rather on all that he—or any person—could become. Fueled by the opportunities that came his way, his life was a testament to his greatness.

At the end of his life, when he'd recognized and accepted that death was coming, Howard's main focus was on one goal:

to take care of his wife—me! And that, in a way, was simply a culmination of all that he had become. Now that he is gone and I can see him for all that he was, my feelings for him have moved forward right along with my life. My passion for him has moved toward respect. Similarly, my passion for life has moved toward gratitude. Without his hand to guide me on a daily basis, I am more respectful than ever of the choices that animated his life and ours. I move forward with a new appreciation of Howard for what he was and remains: a great man.

CHAPTER TWO

THE JOURNEY FORWARD BEGINS

"The bitterest tears shed over graves are for words left unsaid and deeds left undone."

—Harriet Beecher Stowe

AT THE CEMETERY

Howard had expressed a wish that his funeral be very small, so only five of us—his closest family members—attended. Once he'd been interred and everyone else had returned to their cars, I found myself alone with him for the first time and was finally able to speak to him in private.

I approached his grave and looked down at the top of the plain wood coffin, adorned only by a simple Jewish star. This was where I would be leaving my soul mate. I got down on my knees and spoke quietly.

"Howard, I get it. We still have things to do, but . . ."

At that moment, Robert Frost was by my side, sharing the moment and some words from his poem titled "Stopping by Woods on a Snowy Evening." Did I speak them aloud or only think them? "But I have promises to keep. / And miles to go before I sleep."

I rose, brushed the dirt from my hands, and walked away.

A week later, at the end of the traditional Jewish mourning period, I left my daughter's home for my own in Miami. As I gingerly opened the front door and walked into a house that was now mine alone, I recalled Frost's words once more. I had miles to go before I could sleep, and it was time to get started.

For a long time, it seemed I did everything in slow motion. I was fortunate to have a great deal of support from friends and family—and, most important, from Howard himself. He remained very much with me, and whatever I accomplished was with his help. We were still in it together. There's a line of a poem in the film *The Shape of Water* that explains this feeling well: "Unable to perceive the shape of you, I find you all around me. Your presence fills my eyes with your love. It humbles my heart, for you are everywhere."

THE BENCH AND THE TREE

One day while Howard was taking a bath, enjoying the respite from pain that the buoyancy of the water afforded him, he told me he hoped that after his death, a bench and a tree might be placed near his grave. He knew I would come to visit, and he thought the bench would be a comfort to me. As for the tree, it never ceased

to amaze me that a Brooklyn boy would be so enamored of nature—but he most certainly was, right up to the end.

In keeping with Jewish tradition, I waited a year to install the
items he'd requested, during which time my daughter and I were
forced to bring low beach chairs and park them graveside. These
visits were often marred by bugs and blistering sun, making that
bench and tree all the more precious once they were there. Sitting
beside my daughter on Howard's bench, shaded by Howard's tree,
I am perennially reminded of the many ways my husband is still
taking care of me.

Netti related a similar experience of the significance of nature
in communing with her departed mate. Her husband, Wilbur, was
cremated, and his remains—along with a few locks of her hair—
were interred in a mausoleum surrounded by beautiful rocks and
running water. She marveled at the sense of peace and tranquility
these provided for her, thus facilitating her connection to him.
"When I sit at home, I miss Wilbur terribly," she explained, "but
when I sit near him at the cemetery, his essence is with me."

I buried Howard in a cemetery in Naples, Florida, according to his
wishes, though I'd have preferred to keep him closer to Miami,
where I live. (In all honesty, I'd have been content to bury him in
our backyard!) When I asked him why he insisted on Naples, he
offered a simple reason: it would be easier for our daughter, Mara,
to visit him and, ultimately, both of us (because, of course, I would
eventually rest next to him). So be it. At that point in his life, I
would have acquiesced to anything.

In fact, the cemetery proved a perfectly fine choice in spite of
the two hours it would take me to get there. For a while, the ride
provided time for a good cry. Today, I mainly think about how
much nicer that backyard solution would have been. I could have
simply wandered out with my morning coffee, recited a prayer,

and gone back in to take care of the house in all the ways Howard valued.

When Hurricane Irma threatened to batter Miami, Mara and her husband, Tracey, insisted that I come to Naples and stay with them—an excellent idea . . . until the storm changed its mind and descended directly on Naples! *Ah, well*, I thought, *at least we are together*—until it hit me that Howard's coffin might float up from under the ground. I decided right then and there that if that were to happen, I'd insist on packing him into Tracey's truck and taking him home.

"Whatever you need, Mom," my son-in-law replied, clearly bemused. And later, since both he and my daughter are attorneys, they did feel it necessary to share that my plan wasn't exactly legal. Luckily, no such opportunity presented itself (but I do still wish he were here at home, where he belongs).

Like Netti, **Paulina** chose cremation for her wife, Teri—then spent many months agonizing over what to do with her remains. After a year, she was ready to move forward with a plan. Because she and Teri had spent many happy days on their boat, she'd decided to spread her mate's ashes over the ocean they loved. She enlisted a friend to help her carry this out, and once the deed was done, Paulina felt as if a weight had been lifted. "I finally knew that Teri was at peace—at home in the ocean," she told me. "I could begin to move toward my own happiness, just as she would have wanted."

IT'S THE LITTLE THINGS . . . EVEN IN THE CEMETERY

For the first four years after Howard died, my daughter and I visited him together. Although I don't think of myself as particularly "mystical," I'd like to share a few of the moments during which we felt his presence.

In the first year after Howard's death, Mara and I sat near him one day, talking about his love of trees, his garden, and the local birds. He'd always maintained an impressive bird feeder and observed the species it attracted with great fondness. As we sat in silence for a moment, lost in our thoughts, a flock of birds flew over us, singing away—almost speaking, or so it seemed. We looked up, then at each other, and Mara whispered, "He's here! Don't say a word."

What could I say?

On another occasion, gardeners were hard at work when we arrived at the cemetery, laboring to make the area look absolutely lovely and welcoming. Mara and I had the same thought at the same time: Howard would have loved these verdant surroundings nearly as much as he loved his own garden.

On yet another visit, we decided to look at the gravestones surrounding Howard's. What we discovered surprised both of us. The names on the nearby stones eerily resembled those of people Howard had known throughout his life: a neighbor in Brooklyn, a friend who had died young, my mother, his aunt.

And then there was the day the rain blew in as we sat there, the type of Florida rain that comes quickly and in torrents. We had no choice but to run for the car and wait for the storm to abate. Eventually it did, and we headed back to Howard—only to be drenched once more. At that point, Mara said a warp-speed Mourner's Kaddish, and we got out of there, figuring that Howard was telling us in no uncertain terms to go home!

In addition to these moments of communion, there have been a few other funny experiences—and I mean funny-*strange* as well as funny-*humorous*. For those of you who remember the movie *Steel Magnolias*, you know that in the midst of the most horrific moment in one's life, there can be a moment when something happens that serves as a catalyst for almost insane, uncontrollable laughter. When one of the characters is overwhelmed by tears, another creates a split second of unplanned humor. You just have to laugh while you are still crying.

I had three such moments. At the end of the funeral, when I was alone with Howard, as I previously described, I had no idea that the rabbi and the director of the cemetery were standing nearby, observing me. What they saw was me moving from my chair in order to kneel next to his open grave. Perhaps afraid that I'd jump in and join my husband, they came charging down the path, making noises like squawking geese. I reassured them I was fine and just wanted to spend a few minutes more with Howard. They walked away—reluctantly—but continued to observe me from afar.

Sometime within the fourth year after Howard died, my daughter and I were on our way to the cemetery. Having skipped breakfast in favor of getting her two girls off to school, Mara asked if I'd mind stopping off to get some coffee and bagels from Starbucks.

While I was as eager as usual to get to Howard, I wanted to take care of my child's needs first. (Mothers never stop wanting to do that.)

"Mommy," she said as we paid for our food, "do you want to wait, and share breakfast with Daddy?"

I replied quite honestly, "Honey, it has been four long years since I've had a cup of coffee with your dad. Let's do it! We can even share the bagel with him!"

The two of us sat on the bench and unlidded our coffees. Mara split the bagel in two, handed me the more generous portion, and I held it aloft.

"Here you go, Howard," I said. "You can have the half with the most cream cheese!"

Just as I said it, a woman walked past and observed our little ceremony. After hastily attending to her business at a nearby gravesite, she raced back to her car and screeched away. I can only imagine the story she told others about the crazy women at the cemetery, trying to share their picnic with a dead man.

On the fifth anniversary of Howard's death, my daughter and I sat on our bench, sharing our thoughts and reflections. Within ten minutes of our arrival, a multitude of powerful sprinklers emerged from the ground and proceeded to drench us. For a few moments we remained rooted to our spot, but as our clothes began to cling to our bodies, we reluctantly retreated to a dry bench a little ways off to wait for the sprinklers to complete their cycle. However, they showed no sign of letting up.

After a few minutes, Mara looked at me and in a gentle voice, said, "Mom, . . . I believe Daddy is trying to tell us that he wants some peace. He doesn't want to hear any more of our conversation right now."

Hmm, maybe that's where the phrase "rest in peace" comes from, I thought.

"You know what, honey?" I said. "You go on ahead to the car. I want to say goodbye to your father."

She did as I asked while I braved the spray from the sprinklers once more.

I sank to my knees on the wet ground and said, "Howard, it is now five years, and I have tried to do all that you wanted me to. I think there is nothing left to do now but *live*."

With a serene but bittersweet smile, I got to my feet, walked to the car, and we left. I believed then and I know now that I had completed my journey with Howard. Matters of the house were under control, the children had moved on with their lives, and I sensed he was proud of me. It was time to continue on without him.

I want to end this chapter with a story **Mary** told me. In Japanese culture, a kind of secondary funeral is performed after one year. Initially, when Bruce died, Mary gave each of her five children a small portion of his ashes and instructed them to dispose of these remains in their own way. At the end of the first year, the children came from near and far and gathered at her home, where she had arranged for a ceremony in her late husband's beloved garden. There, Mary gave each a small portion of the remaining ashes and asked them to spread these throughout the garden. If they chose, they could say a few words.

While this was going on, Mary's young grandchildren, who had been playing in another part of the garden, saw their parents tossing the ashes and decided to join the action. They began spreading ashes throughout, not understanding the significance of what was happening. All the adults just stopped and stared.

"I didn't know whether to laugh or cry," Mary remembered, "so I just told everyone that I was going inside to make lunch!"

I guess food is a mother's natural response to life's challenges. When in doubt, feed your family!

CHAPTER THREE

CHOICES MADE THROUGHOUT MY PROCESS

**"One's philosophy is not best expressed in words;
it is expressed in the choices one makes."**

—Eleanor Roosevelt

Whether you believe that everything that happens in life is preordained or that we are in control of our destiny, the onset of disease and death probably feels well beyond your control. That doesn't mean you should abandon all efforts to plan ahead. Planning—even in the face of something you cannot ultimately control—can help you move forward step by step. Never mind the *why* of what's happening; stick with the *what,* and just keep doing what you can on a daily basis to keep progressing along the path in front of you. The choice is yours.

You may not have given it much thought when your spouse was alive, but we all make decisions and choices every day. They are necessary for moving forward in life. There's no question that the process gets harder when we find ourselves without a partner, but we can't just stop.

I made many choices and decisions during the five years following Howard's death—and what drove them was all that I'd learned from Howard during our transition period. Uppermost in his mind had been his plan to teach me to do the things he had taken care of throughout our marriage. He'd wanted to make sure things would progress smoothly for me, that I wouldn't be overwhelmed and make the wrong moves. His forethought made my decision-making infinitely easier.

Lorraine provided me with a new perspective on decision-making. She told me that she'd consciously chosen not to blame anyone for her choices after she lost her husband. She believed her path was up to her, and even when she made mistakes, she found solace in the fact that her choices were her own. As she put it, "We can't waste time fretting over the consequences of conscious choices. We can only learn from them and move on."

Anusuya shared with me that in India, after she was widowed, people insisted she needed to be around others constantly so that they could prop her up. She'd found it difficult to explain that this was not what she wanted—or, at least, not *all* the time.

Some of her initial choices included simplifying her life and spending more time on her own, in spite of the cultural traditions she was up against. "I told people about these goals, and said that if there was something I had that they valued, they should just come and get it," she explained. "Really, the only thing I cherished and wanted to hold on to were my books. And, if I felt like living on nothing but sandwiches, I figured that was OK too. Of course, that desire lasted only a little while, and then I realized I wanted to make better choices for the sake of my health. I began eating well and exercising . This was all part of my process of moving forward."

My own first-year choices took hold without a lot of conscious thought. They began simply as an effort to get all of the things repaired that had gone unattended while Howard was ill. After all, I had to make sure the house didn't flood during the rainy season and the wood didn't rot all around me. These were just a couple of things that needed attention within the first few months.

The process of taking care of these and other household things required more effort than I could have imagined, so I found myself organizing the tasks over the course of a year. I'm sure someone else could have gotten everything done faster, but I needed to proceed in a peaceful, methodical way; I needed to give myself permission to take my time.

As Year One reached its conclusion, I began to think about Year Two. It didn't take me long to realize that my next set of choices must involve taking care of all the business matters and paperwork that had accumulated. For starters, a new will had to be drawn up, and our bank accounts and property titles had to be put in my name alone. There were so many other matters as well. Once again, it would take me a full year to accomplish the on-paper "transitions" that had to be made.

Year Three, I decided, would be devoted to clearing the house of everything that was no longer useful, and organizing what I'd decided to keep. This included consolidating and scanning photographs, getting rid of old furniture, and decluttering the many nooks and crannies I'd neglected during Howard's illness.

At some point, people close to me began to ask, "What's on the agenda for next year?"—and I realized that my scheme had taken on a life of its own. At the same time that my "day job" was providing me with stimulation and a modicum of a social life, my yearly goals were giving me a means by which to progress through my new life with purpose. There would never be a morning when I woke up with no reason to get out of bed.

Everything was a choice, and I chose to fill my life with things that needed doing. This is how I moved forward. Although I tended to keep my own counsel, I knew that there were people I could rely on if I needed advice. I found that if I moved forward with confidence, life would send me the right people at the right time—and having this support system was invaluable, even if I didn't call upon it every day.

THE CHOICE TO STAY IN MY HOME

Shortly after Howard died, people began asking me when I would be selling the house. They assumed I would do this, so it was just a question of when. Surely, it was too big and too hard to take care of for one person alone. The extent of the property, the expense of maintaining it . . . all of this would be too much for me.

I knew my friends and family meant well, so I simply thanked them for their concern, smiled, and vowed to spend time thinking about it.

To move or not to move? Although I didn't realize it at the time, this major decision would underlie every other one I would make. I knew I didn't want to leave my home out of fear. It was the source of my strength and comfort, a place where I found peace and staved off confusion. The question was, could I stay? Could I pull it off? The answer was, I'd never know if I didn't try.

At the time, it seemed like a daring decision—so I was fascinated to learn that of the thirteen women I interviewed, eleven chose to stay in their homes. That isn't to say it was an easy decision for any of them—or for me—but clearly, they followed their instincts, just as I did, and relied on themselves to figure out the rest as they went along.

The first time my daughter and I walked through the door after Howard died, she blurted out, "My heavens, Mom, he's all over the house! Everything here is about your life together, your trips, your moments!"

And so it was. My long and happy marriage shouted at me from every corner, every piece of art, knickknack, photograph, and furnishing. Howard was so very present in that house—and not just Howard, but also the two of us together.

If I didn't plan to run away from it, I'd have to acknowledge it. I'd have to accept and make peace with the many memories and mementos of my journey with Howard. Those memories were our story, and keeping the house meant embracing it.

THE CAROUSEL HORSE

As I continued to contemplate the prospect of staying put, various experiences came to mind. The first had to do with a carousel horse that sits in my kitchen. You might wonder how we ended up with such a thing. To explain it, I have to go back to when I was an eight-year-old, living with my family in Queens. We'd just moved from Manhattan into an apartment complex there that backed up to a park with ball fields, a track, and ponies for children to ride on Saturdays and Sundays. There was also an enormous, colorful carousel, and I loved it. Its inviting music could be heard throughout the park, and never failed to make me happy. Riding that carousel formed some of my most cherished memories, right up until I left home at age twenty.

One of the first things I wanted to do with Howard, when we were just getting to know each other, was share with him the way that carousel had made me feel. As our relationship deepened, we'd venture to Central Park for long walks and ice cream, and we'd always end the day with a carousel ride.

Cut to the future—our fifties—when our children had gone off to college and we began to travel. When we visited Paris, I discovered that European carousels were more whimsical than their American counterparts, featuring not just wooden horses, but also elephants, roosters, pigs, and other animals. Our trip would not have been complete without a ride on each one we encountered.

A couple of years after Howard died, while on a work trip to Cincinnati, Ohio, I took a walk downtown with my friend Bud, and there I saw it: a beautifully detailed and ornate carousel whose vibrant music and deep colors beckoned me as it spun round and round. I gathered the courage to tell Bud that I wanted to take a ride, and we did. Afterward, we went for ice cream at Graeter's, Cincinnati's most famous ice cream shop, where I ate a large cup of Black Raspberry Chocolate Chip. It brought back memories of my childhood experiences and later ones with Howard. Now I'd have yet another one to add to those.

As Bud and I laughed and enjoyed our ice cream, I realized something important. I knew in that moment that even without Howard by my side, I would be able to enjoy the things in life that are precious to me. I would be able to continue forming sweet memories, and I could incorporate them into my life's journey along with all those precious moments from the past.

But I am getting ahead of my story, which is about how a carousel horse came into my life. While traveling through Maine on vacation, Howard and I saw something that prompted us to stop the car abruptly and gape in awe. Arrayed on the lawn in front of an old house were all kinds of life-size animal sculptures, including a number of carousel horses. Howard looked at me in amazement. I had always wanted a merry-go-round horse to add to our unusual art collection, but they'd always proved too expensive.

As we sat in wonder, the sound of voices prompted us to look up and see a young couple sitting on the balcony of the house.

"Are these items for sale?" Howard shouted up to them.

In response, the couple started giggling.

"Come back tomorrow after ten," the man called out. "We're closed."

Given the pervasive smell of marijuana in the air, we surmised the two were high as kites.

When we returned the next morning, the young woman explained that the carousel horses were copies, hand carved in Asia, and could be shipped anywhere. The price they quoted was about 10 percent of what we had been quoted over the years for originals.

As we were completing the sale, another piece caught my eye—a beautiful rooster, similar to some we'd seen on carousels in Europe. We talked it over and decided we could only afford one, so we chose the horse and said goodbye to the rooster.

The story would have one more chapter.

Several years later, during the winter, Howard was driving through the Florida Keys when he called me and said, "You won't believe this! I am sitting here in front of a yard covered with huge carved animals! One is the same rooster we saw up in Maine!"

"How amazing!" I replied.

"Well . . . maybe not as amazing as you think. I'm looking at the same couple who sold us the horse, only now they're sitting on beach chairs—and they're just as stoned!"

It turned out that these two spent their summers in Maine and their winters in Key Largo. In short order, we became the owners of that rooster and reunited it with its old friend, the horse.

Why do I bring up this nutty story now? Because, as I contemplated whether or not to sell my house, I realized that if I did, I'd have to get rid of the animals, as they would no doubt be too big for any place I might end up. I wasn't ready to do that—and I'm still not ready! They are simply too important a part of our home—our story—and a daily reminder of the many ways Howard found to make me happy.

THE WOODEN SIGN, LA CUISINE A' ARLENE

Another experience that came to mind in those days of contemplating a move also involved travel. Howard and I loved car trips—stopping whenever we felt like it, drinking coffee and chatting away, sometimes missing exits and ending up on roads less traveled. On one of these excursions, in the Canadian countryside of Charlevoix, north of Montreal—where everything was *très* French—we happened upon an ice cream shop with a *Grand Opening* banner out front. Knowing how much I love my ice cream, Howard pulled up and parked.

Never in our lives had we tasted better ice cream, and I mean *never*. Chocolate is my favorite, and this chocolate was creamy and deep with flavor. Howard was more of a vanilla, butter pecan, and coffee guy (I never said he was perfect), and his choice was so good, he insisted on going back for seconds.

"Really?" I said, raising an eyebrow. "OK, you go for it, but forget about dinner!"

He so enjoyed that second portion that he suggested thirds—at which point I put my foot down and we began a good-natured argument about it. We were interrupted by the sound of banging over our heads.

Perched at the top of a ladder, a man was hanging a beautiful wooden sign festooned with ice cream cones carved in deep relief, its colorful letters outlined in gold. He was attaching it to the wall of the shop with a heavy black metal hanger. We had never seen anything like it.

It turned out that the man was a local artist named Jean-Guy, and we spent some time talking to him about his work. When Howard asked him whether he might be open to creating something for our house, the two of them walked over to the back of his truck to look through his portfolio.

Before too long, the two men had created a sketch for a sign that read *La Cuisine d'Arlene*—Arlene's Kitchen, but with a sweeter ring to it. We made plans to come to his shop the next day, which would involve an excursion to an island by car and ferry. Jean-Guy probably figured he'd never see the couple from Miami again, but that would be to underestimate Howard and me, and the fact that my happiness was Howard's foremost goal in life.

It was pouring rain as we rode that ferry over rough water, but the coffee was strong and hot, and we were not to be deterred.

The sign currently lives happily in my kitchen. Who knows whether it would fit as nicely in another home? I only know it remains an integral part of this one.

THE MIDAS TOUCH

For years, Howard and I traveled to New York City every July, when most residents had fled to various beaches and left the city quieter than usual and easier to navigate. We always included a trip to the SoHo neighborhood of Manhattan, where we'd wander in and out of art galleries. We both happened to like bronzes, and on one visit, Howard became enamored of a Charles Bragg sculpture titled *Midas,* depicting a crotchety old man with a greedy smirk, hunched over stacks of coins and other symbols of wealth. How my husband loved that sculpture!

About two weeks after returning home, Howard called me from his office and announced that he had purchased crotchety old *Midas.* I was astounded. Remember, I had known Howard since he was seventeen years old, and he had never acted on impulse in quite this way. To be clear, I had no problem at all with owning a piece Howard had so admired. But in all our years together, my husband had never spent a significant sum on something without consulting me. We always discussed large purchases and made a joint decision.

I couldn't help expressing my shock, and his response was to assume I didn't like the sculpture.

It was a rare moment when we talked at cross-purposes until finally, I said, "Fine. This is a new experience for me. I understand now that we may sometimes make decisions independently, and I will take that into account in the future."

My response had clearly shaken Howard. When he got home that evening, he apologized, said he had made a mistake in ordering the sculpture, and told me he had canceled the purchase.

"Thank you," I said. "I appreciate that." But I knew what I would do. It took me several months to save up the money, but by April, just in time for his birthday, *Midas* was delivered.

Howard just smiled when he opened the parcel and said, "I guess that argument was never about the piece."

"No," I responded, "it was about us!"

Truth be told, I never really loved *Midas,* but today he is as precious to me as anything I own.

THE BRANCHES AND THE DUMPSTER

One January evening, Howard and I went to a nice Italian restaurant and left well-fed and content. We had parked in a lot behind the restaurant, where the dumpsters from it and several other establishments sat. Protruding from one of them were what appeared to be tall, white and silver tree branches made of wood—probably remnants of Christmas decor. I pointed them out to Howard.

"Those would be perfect in our big vases," I said excitedly, referring to some multitiered vessels I'd left empty, hoping to come upon the right thing with which to fill them.

"Don't tell me you want to plunge into that dumpster to get them!" he exclaimed. (We wouldn't hear the term *dumpster diving* until years later.)

"That's exactly what I'm telling you!" I cried, and out of the car we jumped.

Howard climbed right into the dumpster while I hung over the side, and we managed to retrieve our treasure.

The branches were too big to fit in the car and they hung over the edge of the trunk, making it impossible to close. Undeterred, we set off slowly and carefully, traveling over local streets, praying we'd get home with ourselves and our acquisition intact.

When we got home, we enlisted our friend's son Greg, who was visiting us from California, to help us bring the branches inside.

As he labored, he kept shaking his head and mumbling, "You are the only people I know who go out for a simple dinner and come back with trash from a dumpster!"

It wasn't trash to us. Howard understood that for me, having art (although sometimes in odd forms) within our home improved the quality of our life. I believe art is like an iceberg in that you see the tip but not what is below—especially not the story.

THE LAMPS

This next story of the lamps reinforces what Howard did in order to bring beauty into my life and our home.

Howard and I had experienced challenges on a flight once on Eastern Airlines (which is no longer in business). As a result, the airline awarded us two free flights to anywhere in the contiguous United States. We chose San Francisco, as that was as far as we could travel from Miami, and we had never been there. Actually, at that time, we had never been *anywhere* far from home.

On our first evening in San Francisco, we walked around Ghirardelli Square and came upon a restaurant with a sign in front that read *Auction Tonight*. We had always loved auctions, so we knocked on the door. It was opened by some workers who stated that we had missed the auction, as it had taken place the previous evening. However, they kindly allowed us to come in to take a peek.

As soon as we stepped inside, we saw them: the most breathtaking, large, richly colored stained glass lamps our eyes had ever beheld. We just stood and stared at them. Howard spoke with the workers, who happened to know the identity of the person who had bought the lamps, and they gave us her name. To our surprise, the purchaser was the designer/decorator for Tavern on the Green, a very famous restaurant in New York City.

After placing many calls to locate her phone number, Howard finally spoke with her. She agreed to meet us at the restaurant several weeks later, as we already had plans to go to New York. We met, and she provided us with a tour of the iconic restaurant set in the middle of Central Park, with its manicured greenery and horse-drawn carriages outside to greet all those entering the restaurant.

She explained that the owner did not wish to sell any of the lamps purchased at the auction in San Francisco, as he had bought them as replacements for similar ones hanging in the restaurant's entryway. She was so impressed with our perseverance in locating her and how enamored we were with the beauty of the lamps, she gave us the name of the artist, Val Sigstedt, who both created and repaired them.

The artist was located in Point Pleasant, Pennsylvania, along the Delaware River. As one might expect upon having learned of our tenacity, we tracked him down, and off we went to Pennsylvania. Val, who we were delighted to discover looked just like Willie Nelson, was kind enough to spend hours with us. As he modestly explained to us that he was a "colorist," we recognized we were in the presence of true creativity and a master creator in the art of stained glass.

While the lamps at Tavern on the Green were over three feet in diameter, we could only manage to afford one that was thirty-three inches. But we were thrilled. The lamp took Val six months to make, and he kindly allowed us to make bimonthly payments.

Finally, it came time to transport the lamp from Val's shop in Pennsylvania to our home in Florida. As the lamp was composed of hundreds of small pieces of fragile glass, we were concerned it might break in transit. We also had to figure out how to hang it and how to electrically connect it. Who knew the answers to all these concerns? Certainly not us. We were relieved to hear Val explain that we were not to worry; he personally would deliver it to us. Little did we know, he drove a Mazda RX-7, which is actually quite small, but we placed our faith in him. Our job was to prepare scaffolding, provide Val with the schematics of the house, and hire an electrician to assist him. Fortunately, we had become friends with the architect/builder of our house, who volunteered to help, so the arrangements were made. The lamp was installed over the long Thanksgiving weekend.

Howard and I sat under that lamp for many years, chatting away and never tiring of admiring its beauty each evening.

A period of twelve years went by, during which the children graduated from college. One night, as we sat bathed in the lamp's extraordinary glow, Howard said to me, "I would really like that thirty-nine-inch lamp that we originally could not afford." I was thrilled by the prospect and privilege of purchasing a second lamp. So a repeat experience occurred, lamp number two was designed. Val delivered this one as well. We hung this lamp in our kitchen over a small island, and most evenings we sat quietly under it, sipping our café very slowly. The panes of various blues and purples shimmered above us as we gazed upward; then, as we turned to look into the family room, we'd see the original lamp illuminating panes of red and pink. Those beautiful colors, shining in contrast to the black night outside the windows, were thrilling to us, as they increased our appreciation of the moment and our gratitude for the life we shared every day and every night.

Now, by myself, as I close down the house each evening, I leave those lamps glowing. While walking from the kitchen, past the family room, toward my bedroom, I look up and say, "Good night, Howard . . . thank you," and I smile.

The 33" lamp which we purchased first.

The 39" lamp we bought after the kids went to college.

Two of the other widows, **Donna** and **Mary**, also referred to specific items in their homes that provided support for their emotional move forward. Donna explained that as she and Ray had owned an antique shop for fifteen years, several of their favorite antiques had made their way into their home. In fact, sometimes they'd end up buying one thing for the store and two things for the house. Donna shared that these specific antiques brought back memories from which she drew great comfort. She explained that the familiarity they exude serves as a bridge between an important part of her life and the present, and that this brings her peace.

Mary keeps an entire room of Bruce's things; she calls it the "junk room." This was his den and still has lots of his stuff in it. "Whenever I find something that was his, it goes right into the junk room," she explained.

"Of course," I responded, "because that's where Bruce is. It's still his room."

Several of my fellow widows reflected upon issues of *home*—what their homes meant to them in the aftermath of their loss, and why they decided to stay (or, in some cases, go).

Kelly had a variety of decisions to make in the first year of her widowhood. Taking care of major house issues wasn't as alien to her as it was to me, as she had been the one to manage various contractors over the years. But she soon discovered that as a woman alone, she was being taken advantage of. The workers she hired simply weren't doing as good a job as they should have been doing. "It was hard," she told me, "but I just had to pull myself together, fire these guys, and replace them with contractors I could trust. In the end, I earned the respect of the people who worked for me, and I salvaged my self-respect as well. Plus, the work was done right!"

Harder for Kelly to deal with was her sense that her husband's spirit inhabited the house throughout that first year, and then disappeared—no doubt as a result of her becoming more independent and successful on her own. Ultimately, she accepted this as part of her journey and learned to take comfort in the idea that he no longer "needed" to stick around.

Only one of the women, **Donna**, told me that she'd received nothing but full support and encouragement to stay where she was for as long as she felt safe and functional there. I think this can be chalked up to the unusual community in which she lives: Benicia, California. Apparently, Benicia is one of those rare places where the term *community* is taken to heart. People take care of one another there, especially those who are older and/or alone. Community members work together to provide the specific assistance others need, whether physical or emotional, making it easier for older or single people to remain in their homes for as long as they want to.

Intrigued by the stories Donna told about the place, I arranged to visit with members of the community at their weekly Friday-night wine-and-pizza gathering. They explained that they had been helping one another out for decades and believed it was everyone's responsibility to provide encouragement and assistance to each member of the group. They shared that members of the Benicia community worked together to help people remain in their own homes for as long as they wished to do so. They arranged to drive seniors to food stores, medical appointments, and social gatherings. They supported each individual's active participation in community activities by including them whenever possible and making sure they had a means of safe transportation. If only more communities followed this model, fewer widows would have to face the prospect of leaving homes that had sheltered and nurtured them for decades.

In the aftermath of Howard's death, I came to understand the saying, "Advice is criticism in a cashmere sweater." Friends and family, as well-meaning as they are, can press advice on us that we are not ready to hear. Being told you should move "for your own good" can be overwhelming. A house isn't just a place to live, and things aren't just *things*. They are memories that connect us to moments in our lives, happy times we've enjoyed, and people who were and are important to us. They ground us and give us strength during transitional times—and there is nothing more transitional than widowhood. Sometimes we need the comfort of familiar surroundings to grow, and there is no shame in that.

Netti shared with me that, because their house was 140 years old, she and her husband always believed there were essences of others in it. Today, she believes that while Wilbur no longer lives with her there, the memories they made remain. "When I feel the need to be close to him, I sit under our prayer blanket," she told me, "or in the chair he liked to sit in while he was sick." She has no intention of getting rid of those things. Why would she?

Mary has remained in the home she shared with Bruce since 1969, and, although selling it and moving might seem logical from a financial standpoint, she loves it. In addition to enjoying the house itself, she enjoys her neighborhood and access to the city of San Francisco. At age eighty-one, she remains strong and in good health, so she is constantly on the go—at least, for now. She is aware that eventually she may have to give up the house, but she's just not ready to do so at this point.

Barbara and Butch built their house together. After he died, she was advised by a friend from Holland that in her country, when a spouse dies, friends come into the home and rearrange the furniture so the widow will no longer look around, expecting her husband to be there. "The idea is that furniture and objects can trigger the expectation of someone's presence," Barbara explained. She followed this plan to some degree. She moved a bench and rotated certain objects, but she still believes it is their house—hers and Butch's. It isn't that she expects him to appear, but she feels his presence and accepts it as part of her process.

When I spoke to **Sara,** she reflected upon the fact that since childhood, she has liked living in the country, near the mountains, in a small town. "My paternal grandmother had a garden where I spent time growing and picking fruits," she said. A year and a half after becoming a widow, Sara moved back to her farm. She believes it served as her foundation for moving forward. "That farm is my comfort zone," she told me. "Its consistency has been like a bridge, though I've modernized it a bit." I imagine that the process of modernizing an eighteenth-century farmhouse has given Sara a particular kind of stability, just as my own work on my house has done for me.

One change that Sara particularly wanted to make was adding huge windows to one side of the house, creating a room where plants could thrive. She can now be indoors while enjoying the outdoors she loves. Her family life continues as she creates new memories on a foundation of old ones. Congratulations, Sara, and welcome home!

The choice of remaining in a marital home after widowhood—or not—affects a world of other choices every woman in this position must make. **Donna** recognizes the realities of being an octogenarian, and still isn't sure exactly how she'll move forward. She does know that she has to plan for a time when she can't do everything on her own—but for now, although yard work has become more difficult and the stairs seem steeper, when she looks around, she loves what she sees. All she can do is move forward one step at a time.

Like me, **Netti** had to face a lot of well-meaning people who asked her, "Why are you staying in that big house?" Some days, she finds it hard to answer. "It isn't because *we* lived here," she told me. "I understand that the house is mine alone; it will always be my home. *I* live here."

She has thought about the fact that she could live exclusively on the first floor if necessary, and told me that she keeps two lists: Reasons to Stay and Reasons to Leave. "If Wilbur were alive, we'd discuss it, she said, "but as things are, I have to evaluate the situation by myself. Lists make it easier for me. The other thing that makes it easier is that the house is finally all paid for; I made the last payment in December."

During one of my later visits with **Kelly**, she suggested that I add the following to thoughts about making decisions regarding one's home: "No widow should make any permanent life decisions, especially things like moving or selling a house, for at least two years. This may not be possible financially, but I do think it's optimal. I think that's the amount of time it takes to get to the point where you can make thoughtful, careful choices that will be good for the long haul."

Several of the other women and I chose to accomplish a number of essential tasks over our first few years of widowhood to facilitate our staying in our homes. For example, although **Sallie** realized that she had never managed their finances, and she needed to get help and guidance in this area, a more immediate issue she had to tackle (as hurricane season would be coming, and she lived alone) was the enormous challenge of learning about the installation of a house generator as well as hurricane shutters. If she wanted to stay in her house during the approaching hurricane season, this hill had to be climbed. As she put it, "It became a part of my plan to stay in my house as a way of moving forward."

Netti was able to survive the floods of Cincinnati the first year after Wilbur died, yet gradually, over two years, she began her process of taking care of home repairs as they were needed—including such large undertakings as the roof and driveway. In a way, she did what I did, though without the predetermined goal of getting it accomplished within a year. She made a list and started checking things off as they needed to be done. As of our last meeting, the list still had a number of items unchecked, and it probably always will, as she continues to add to it.

Paulina waited till Year Two before repainting in order to introduce lighter colors and purchasing a new living room set. She hoped the lighter colors would bring a new lightness to her mood as well as her decor, and that is exactly what happened.

At this point, I thought it might be useful to share a fuller list of what I embarked upon over the five-year period following Howard's death. Of course, your list will be different; mine is simply an example. However you choose to prioritize the many seemingly overwhelming tasks ahead of you in the wake of your spouse's death, getting organized can tame your fears and provide a road map that will help guide you through the new territory ahead. And don't forget to celebrate each accomplishment! Recognition of your successes is an integral part of the process of moving forward. (Feel free to celebrate your missteps as well. These are the learning experiences that pave the way for more effective choices in the future.)

As I have previously explained, I decided to give myself a full year to accomplish each of the large sets of tasks I set for myself. This gave me the flexibility to make mistakes, stumble, pick myself up, and try again. There were times when I looked in the mirror and laughed—a feeling I shared with **Margaret**, who instantly commiserated and shared a story of her own.

At some point in the first year after Margaret's husband's death, her water heater stopped working. After pressing numerous buttons to no avail, she figured she'd better call a plumber. The problem turned out to be a simple blown-out pilot light—something she could easily have taken care of—but it cost her $100 to find that out. "In an instant, your life changes forever," was how Margaret described widowhood. "Every task in your life is now your responsibility alone—no more partner with whom to share the duties."

I had a similar experience a few weeks after Howard died, when I couldn't get any hot water out of the faucet in the tub. I called the plumber, who looked into the situation and gently informed me that I was turning on the wrong faucet. Price tag for my ignorance: $100. (There must be an official widow's rate for such blunders.) Like Margaret, I laughed, I learned, and I moved on. I never made that mistake again, although I did make others.

Here are some year-by-year specifics, including stories about the all-important support system I developed—professionals I could trust and rely on to do the work I felt unqualified to tackle myself. Occasionally, well-meaning friends would question my choice of a contractor or other helper. "We can find you somebody cheaper," they'd insist. I'd explain that for someone in my position—new to many of the responsibilities now on my shoulders—having dependable professionals who knew me and my house was more important than saving a few dollars. When your life has been disrupted, continuity can be invaluable.

Following is a list of tasks I accomplished during the first year after Howard's death:

Year One

- Replaced the roof, which included learning to review and understand contracts, building permits, and other documents.
- Had the house tented and treated for termites, which had to be done mid-roof installation.
- Repaired the outside lights—seventy-one of them, with the expert help of Edwin, the electrician.
- Had the windows and wood casings painted by Juan Carlos, our trusty painter.
- Filed the annual insurance paperwork.
- Repaired leaks in the pool.
- With the help of four friends, removed Howard's clothes from our closets, along with everything of mine that wasn't black. (The women would return a year later to help me put back the rest of my clothes.)
- Replaced a variety of faucets.
- Arranged for garden maintenance, including landscape cleaning, tree trimming, and cherry picking. (Can you imagine needing cherry pickers?) I would learn that

taking care of the garden is an annual project that, when hurricanes or tropical storms come through, might necessitate the hiring of several people for a duration of months.

Year Two

In Year Two, I recognized two things: First, I needed a break from my endless focus on home repairs (although, of course, I would continue to take care of anything pressing). Second, I was going to have to make some real-life, grown-up financial and business decisions. No longer would Howard and I work through these matters together; I'd be going it alone on budgets, bank accounts, investments, wills, and everything else.

Step 1 would be officially removing his name from our legal documents—or those that hadn't yet been taken care of. Howard had helped me revise the titles on whatever we could get to before he died. The rest required death certificates, which I found myself keeping in the trunk of my car in case they were immediately needed. (At times it felt as though my husband himself were in that trunk!)

Here's a rundown of all that I accomplished in Year Two:

- Upgraded my personal technology, which included purchasing a new Blackberry (the cutting-edge PDA of the time).
- Switched to a different wireless carrier, based on my research into the relative costs and benefits.
- Had a new will and trust drawn up with the help of our family attorney.
- Moved all of our bank accounts, investments, and utility accounts into my name solely.
- Reapplied for a Florida homestead exemption, a state requirement which helps reduce county taxes.

- Replaced our old alarm system with a more up-to-date wireless one.
- Applied for new credit cards in my name alone and deactivated our joint ones.
- Changed air-conditioning companies.
- Arranged for necessary appliance repairs, including the oven.
- Completely remodeled the master bedroom closet to suit my own needs.

Year Three

In Year Three, I turned my attention to the upstairs level of my house—starting with several large pieces of old oak furniture that Howard and I had refinished way back in 1967, before we were even married. Having very little money in those days, our best option had been to buy everything used or very cheap and add our own magic.

Many of those pieces we'd acquired early on—chests, dry sinks, a rolltop desk, etc.—had migrated upstairs and finally outlived their usefulness; it was time to declutter and donate. This turned out to be more complicated than I'd expected. Perhaps you know this already, but it was news to me that even though I intended to give the furniture away, I would be hard-pressed to find anyone willing to carry it downstairs and cart it off. It took my friend Sally, who had come down from New York for her annual "help" visit, to get the job done. She called no fewer than eighteen charities before she found a group willing to take on the task.

The next difficult undertaking in front of me was dealing with several generations of family photos—some seven thousand of them—dating from as far back as the early 1900s and concluding with my journey with Howard through 2013. They ran the gamut from tattered black-and-white snapshots to high-quality color prints.

The sorting process alone took me about three months. By the end of that period, I'd reduced the number of photos by half, mainly by trashing the duplicates. (I sometimes felt as if I were throwing Howard himself in the trash, which was no fun.) I was left with 3,300 pictures to scan, which I packed into several shopping bags and carried to a professional, one bag at a time. I just couldn't face scanning that many images myself. The man in the shop reassured me that I should just keep them coming, joking that I could have a "scanning tab," the way some people have bar tabs.

As a professor for over forty years, I'd accumulated hundreds of books and journals that I kept upstairs in bookcases. I decided that many of these, too, had to go. Believe it or not, I found the books even harder to give away than the furniture. Apparently, in the digital age, printed matter has become unwieldy and, to some people, unnecessary. It would take me a full year to find welcoming homes for the array of textbooks and works of literature I'd so lovingly collected.

Here are the things I accomplished during Year Three, in addition to the furniture, photo, and book projects:

- Familiarized myself with U-verse internet and DirecTV setup.
- Initiated bulky item trash collection to supplement my regular trash pickup.
- Figured out how to navigate numerous computer challenges, including how to return unnecessary items I'd been duped into buying by some dubious personnel at Best Buy.
- Learned how to replace the huge battery in the house alarm.
- Replaced all inside light bulbs with more energy-efficient and cost-effective LED lights.
- Initiated outdoor work necessitated by the replacement of pipes.
- Reviewed, then organized and/or disposed of every piece of paper that had accumulated over the thirty-five years we'd occupied the house.

Year Four

In Year Four, it was time to work on the outside of the house while maintaining the status quo indoors as necessary. This proved extraordinarily challenging—more so than anything I'd tackled up to this point. The things that needed taking care of outside tended to be large-scale projects, requiring the services of outside companies, whose recommendations and estimates confused me. In order to navigate an expensive project such as a complete driveway replacement or waterfall reconstruction, I decided to turn to my son-in-law for help. He took charge of these undertakings, hired folks, and physically worked alongside them. Even so, my head was spinning; without him, I can't even imagine.

Here are the rest of the things I tackled in Year Four:

- Had the walls of the house and pool area pressure-washed.
- Added new exterior lights.
- Replaced rotten wood wherever necessary.
- Recalked the windows.
- Hired tree trimmers and landscapers for the semiannual garden refurbishment.

Year Five

By Year Five, I had completed all pressing household jobs and taken over all of the financial and business responsibilities that Howard had previously handled. But when it comes to a house (and a life), the tasks never seem to end. I continued to address things as they arose, my confidence growing as time passed. Year Five often felt improvisational—as if I were starring in a movie and watching it at the same time. I continually reevaluated my abilities and found myself feeling good about my decision to remain in my home. *Our* home.

Where to live is not the kind of decision others can make for you, and I would urge you to take all the time you need to make it. For me, a five-year period of growth (and fear and mistakes and triumphs) was critical to my sense of well-being about my choice to keep the house. My goal for Year Five became to face anything and everything that presented itself with confidence that I'd find the best solution.

So, what were the "anything and everything" that arose? Here they are:

- Purchased and replaced three air-conditioning units.
- Oversaw the work of several tree-trimming companies.
- Continued to replace rotted wood and rain gutters
- Replaced windows.
- Hired an exterminator to target the back of the house.
- Replaced the filter and motor for the pool.
- Replaced my large flat-screen TV after researching my best options.
- Replaced picture windows with hurricane-resistant glass and altered insurance coverage accordingly.

Since Year Five, naturally, I've continued to take care of all aspects of the house and grounds. With each passing year, I become more confident, more adept, and more level-headed about the problems that arise. I know Howard would be proud to see what I have accomplished and how I have grown—though I am pretty sure he'd say he knew all along I could handle it!

DIFFICULT CHOICES

"Destiny is a name often given in retrospect to choices that had dramatic consequences."
—J. K. Rowling

There are choices some women must make that are even more gut-wrenching than whether or not to stay in their homes. Three of the widows I spoke with recalled distinct challenges they faced well before they lost their husbands.

As Bruce developed dementia over the six years before he died, **Mary** made the decision to send him to a care facility for his own safety. As hard as it was to do, she understood that he had declined to the point where he was no longer the person she'd married. Over time, she'd taken on more and more of the responsibilities of their life. As he slowly left her, she knew her life was changing permanently and did what she had to do to move forward.

Shortly after **Rosalyn** and Ril married, Ril developed kidney disease, which they would battle for seven long years. Additionally, one of their daughters had been born with similar problems. Like Mary, Rosalyn began to take on the bulk of the responsibilities at home. She tried to keep things as normal as possible throughout the end of Ril's life, and then, when he died, she discovered she'd already experienced some aspects of the grieving process. At that point, her goal became to maintain a loving atmosphere for her girls and keep their father alive for them—even if it meant putting her own grief on the back burner.

As Ray's dementia progressed and his own safety became compromised, **Donna** had to make the difficult decision to place him in a convalescent home. She understood that the most loving thing she could do was ensure Ray's safety, but that didn't mean it was easy. After he died, she realized that her loneliness and mourning had begun long before then.

The more I delved into the stories other women shared with me, the less alone I felt. So much of what they told me reflected experiences and feelings I'd had myself. At the same time, each of our stories was unique; our challenges, different; and our ways of coping, singular. We widows together make up a community of diverse individuals, and there is strength in sharing what we have in common as well as what we have done differently.

PERSONAL CHOICES THAT GOT ME THROUGH THE FIRST YEAR

The first year after Howard died, I made three decisions about my personal behavior that I believe helped me move forward. I did not plan them; they just evolved from my innermost feelings and survival instincts. They were to wear only black, not listen to music, and not dance.

Wearing Black

Wearing black is a traditional expression of mourning in many cultures, including our own (though American widows today tend not to adhere to such rigorous customs). I decided this discipline suited me, and immediately moved the rest of my clothes out of my closet. For one year, I'd focus my energies on getting through each day and maintaining my emotional stability—not on what outfit I'd be wearing.

What I soon discovered was that this choice not only freed me from issues of fashion, appearance, and impression; it also set me on a path of simplicity. It became easier to move through the day and, at day's end, drop my simple clothes into the laundry basket, take a hot shower, and climb into bed. When the next day arrived, simplicity prevailed once more. Year One went by in this fashion (or lack of it).

No Music

Whatever era we came of age in—in my case, it was the sixties—we all remember beloved music and lyrics of the day. What's more, throughout the course of a long relationship, certain songs accrue special meaning. Music has a way of evoking memories, moments, and firsts as nothing else can, and producing what's known as a *frisson*—a kind of shiver akin to an electric current.

I knew that getting through all the milestones of Year One—birthdays, anniversaries, and such—would be difficult. I decided it might be easier to weather these occasions without the additional associations and feelings called up by the music that had become meaningful to Howard and me. One of these songs was "Yes, I'm Ready" by Barbara Mason; another was "My Cup Runneth Over" by Ed Ames. Add to those the romantic strains of Johnny Mathis, Roberta Flack, and the rest of the romantic slow-dance music of those years; operatic arias; and Broadway show tunes. Even Hallmark commercial jingles could set off a flood of feelings inside me. So I made a conscious effort to avoid this stimulus during Year One, knowing that eventually, these songs would provide comfort rather than sheer pain.

Once that first year had passed, I allowed myself to experience the impact of music once again. I even had the line "My cup runneth over"—a quote from one of our favorite songs *and* psalms—engraved on the bench near Howard's grave. Music remains integral to my memories of Howard, and that phrase is a concrete testament to the love we shared.

No Dancing

Remembering the shared feelings, the closeness, the touch can be overwhelming. I had often described life with Howard as a dance, so when that dance ended, it made sense for me to take a break from literal dancing. Again, this left me more able to focus on what I needed to accomplish. It also offered me an excuse for declining invitations to parties and gatherings, which spared me the experience of sitting at a table while the music and other couples spun around me. Not attending parties was a beneficial result of my moratorium on music and dancing. My choices fit together, and they fit *me*.

Since I've mentioned it a few times, allow me to share more about the dance. When I was seventeen and in my first year of college, I met Howard in one of my classes. He was quite awkward-looking: very skinny, tall, dark, and not terribly handsome. One Friday, we discovered that we would both be attending the same party that evening. I informed the girls going with me that I knew a boy from class—Howard—who was very nice; perhaps one of them might "like" him.

As it turned out, neither Howard nor I knew anyone else at that gathering with whom we might dance, so he asked me for the first one. He turned out to be a terrific dancer! We ended up dancing the entire evening away (which is what we did in the sixties if we weren't interested in drinking or drugs). We continued dancing through four years of college.

Fast-forward about half a century to that fateful cruise near the end of his life. The first two nights at sea, we sat, having ginger ale in a lounge before dinner while a small trio played soft music.

"I think we should try to dance," Howard said.

"Absolutely!" I replied, and so we did.

Placing my hands on his shoulders, I stood very close as he whispered in my ear, "We began our life dancing, we have always loved to dance, and this may be our last dance—so just hold me up."

I did just that, and, as usual, Howard was right. It was our last dance.

CHAPTER FOUR

THE PEOPLE WE NEED

"Real change, enduring change happens one step at a time."
—Ruth Bader Ginsburg

I'm sure you've heard the adage, "It takes a village to raise a child." Well, it also takes a village to heal a heart. I have come to believe that there are people who are put in our paths for a purpose: to become part of our journey of recovery.

We need other human beings throughout our lives, but never more so than when we are bereaved. Likewise, that is when it is most important to eliminate negative or toxic people and fill in the gaps they leave with valued friends, new and old. It's an important time to take inventory of our relationships, nurture and appreciate the ones that are worthwhile, and eliminate the rest. In my case, I decided that *trust* had to be at the core of every relationship in which I engaged. It became my main criterion for friendship (and I include family in that category as well). The people I came to trust in the wake of Howard's death—male and female—were the ones who went beyond their own needs to embrace the needs of others.

When I asked her about this, **Lorraine** thoroughly agreed with me. "It was so terribly difficult, after John died, to trust anyone as I trusted him," she told me. "But I realized it isn't about that. It's about taking things one step at a time. I just put my faith in the universe and believed that the people I needed would somehow be put in my path."

It meant a lot to me to hear Lorraine and others voice this kind of faith—because I share it, and it describes my experience perfectly. The people I needed—the ones who would help me move forward—did seem to come into my life almost miraculously, and I want to tell you about some of them.

THREE WOMEN

There were three women who were literally by my side when Howard died. These three—Lee, Betty, and Daisy—were there when he drew his final breath and when his body was taken out of our home. They had become integral to our lives during Howard's illness, and when I talked to them later about his death, they each described it similarly, saying that watching me in those moments felt like an out-of-body experience.

Lee had driven Howard and me around when it became too difficult for us to manage it. She'd kept us company—and listened to me endlessly—when Howard could no longer go out much. And she'd spent the night with me after his body was removed from the house. She continued to do everything she possibly could for a very long time, including ferrying me around on errands and simply showing me how much she cared. Her attentiveness persisted for four full years, until her own life changed. At that point, Lee met her soul mate and moved on with him, beginning the wonderful life she truly deserved.

Betty was equally helpful and caring, coming to take over from Lee the morning after Howard died. She brought coffee and croissants, but more important, she brought comfort and genuine concern. After a few weeks, when it was time for me to return to work, Betty drove me there. She continually came up with reasons to get me out of the house—to go to the gym, the beach, or a café. She listened. Eventually, she, too, moved on with her life, as our friends must, but not before she'd given me the valuable gift of her friendship.

Daisy, Howard's "work wife," was also present in his final hours. She'd been the front-desk assistant at his orthodontic practice for twenty-five years and had undoubtedly taken better care of him than anyone other than me. She continued to spend time with me after he was gone, often over coffee, and got me laughing as she told story after story about his exploits at the office. She understood my heartache in a way that no one else did. Perhaps that's why it felt safe to laugh heartily when she suggested that we should have had him stuffed (like Roy Rogers's legendary horse, Trigger, for those of you who remember) and propped him up at his desk. In the evenings, he could be carried home and settled into his favorite chair. A crazy kind of humor, I know, but perhaps less so if you've been married to someone—or worked with him for a long time.

Daisy never really recovered from Howard's death and hasn't managed to find a work situation she feels as happy with. I continue to visit with her over croissants and *café con leche,* and we still laugh and cry over the impact this man had on us.

These three women, all present on that fateful night, have helped keep Howard alive within me and have helped me put him to rest and move forward. The one thing my husband asked of me at the end was that I not forget him—as if I could. These women understand and honor that request, and have helped me retain my sense of humor as well as my dignity. They've helped me retain *Howard.*

TWO ELVES

The next two people I want to talk about are Juan Carlos and Xiomara (pronounced cee-o-MAR-a). They have worked in our home for many years, and are still with me. Juan Carlos takes care of all of the painting and repairs. There have been projects he worked on for months—not unlike the character of Eldin in the old TV series *Murphy Brown*. Howard and I used to joke that Juan Carlos was *our* Eldin. Xiomara comes in several mornings a week to take care of the house and, like Juan Carlos, has come to feel that my house is her house too. (I couldn't be happier that she feels this way.) When a hurricane bears down on us, Juan Carlos checks on me to make sure I have what I need. Xiomara keeps me informed about what we might be running low on, and just generally helps me live a well-ordered, functional life.

But, of all of the many gifts these two have given me, I want to talk about one in particular. I've mentioned that after Howie died, I spent a week at my daughter's, where we mourned and "sat shiva"—the Jewish tradition of gathering after a death. But there came a moment when I had to go home and begin my life without my husband.

When the time came for me to enter the bedroom—our bedroom—I dreaded it. Actually, I feared it, even with my daughter by my side. I knew that the hospice people had been there to remove the hospital bed and other equipment, but there would still be so much disorder, so much evidence of his illness and death. I steeled myself . . . and, to my utter shock and amazement, found everything in perfect order! Juan Carlos and Xiomara, my magic elves, had been there. They had moved the heavy furniture back into place, vacuumed the rugs, and cleaned everything. Our bedroom smelled and looked clean and perfect.

I would find out later that in order to eliminate the stains left behind, my two dear friends had gotten down on their hands and knees and scrubbed the carpet. That is what I mean about embracing the needs of others. What more could one ask of another human being? I am so fortunate to have Juan Carlos and Xiomara in my life.

ONE VALENTINE

I'd like to say something now about the thoughtful efforts of Edwin, our electrician. Like Juan Carlos, Edwin had worked in our home for many years. After Howard died, he was emphatic that I should call him whenever something went wrong. He made it clear that he was offering his friendship as well as his services, and that he never wanted me to be concerned about household problems I might not understand. "I'll come day or night," he insisted, and I believed him.

Edwin has been true to his word. He has done all necessary electrical work quickly and reasonably, but he has also become my advisor on a wide array of other household problems. Whenever anything goes wrong, I know I can call him. He'll come immediately, and if he can't do the work necessary, he'll help me figure out who can.

It had never occurred to me that the various people we'd paid to do work for us over the years would become so essential to both my physical and emotional well-being, but that is exactly what transpired. Before I leave the topic of Edwin, I'll share one gesture that says it all. On the first Valentine's Day after Howard died, Edwin came to my door with a bouquet of flowers. "Doc would not have wanted you to spend Valentine's Day unappreciated, so these are from him," he said, pressing the arrangement into my hands. What could I say but "Thank you, my friend, for being here and for being so understanding."

This past Valentine's Day, Edwin brought me orchids.

OH, YOU'VE GOT TO HAVE FRIENDS

I think of my friend Sally as the "Queen of New York"—one of the most competent, smart, organized, and genuinely good people I know. A few months after Howard died, she showed up on my doorstep, having waited patiently for me to be ready to accept her help. (As patience is not one of Sally's strong suits, I appreciated her restraint in giving me time to regain my equilibrium.)

I don't think either of us was sure what exactly Sally could do for me at that point, but she hit upon the perfect thing. My closet became the fulcrum of her efforts on that initial visit. I've already talked about the task of removing Howard's clothes from our closets, along with temporarily relocating most of my own. I'm sure you understand what a fraught experience it can be, surrounding yourself with the smell, style, and essence of your departed loved one as you banish his things to another place. Having Sally there to help me with the job was simply a godsend.

While he was alive, Howard had spoken to Daisy about making sure that his very fine slacks, shirts, shoes, and other items would go to those who might need and appreciate them. Through her church, Daisy found a deserving family man who had lost his job and needed nice clothing for interviews and new employment. I'm sure Howard's wardrobe gave this man the confidence and style he needed to jump-start his work life and continue taking care of his loved ones.

Ultimately, Sally, Daisy, and Lee would work steadily for seven-and-a-half hours to turn Howard's and my closet into just mine, filled with the simple black garments I'd live in until I was ready to fully resume my life. My women friends respected and supported my decision to wear black for a year—but more than that, they helped me make it happen.

In Year Two, Sally came over again. With the help of the same crew, plus my friend April, she reworked my closet yet again so it became what I now wanted and needed: a beautiful storage space meant for a woman. It took Sally several days to organize the closet by color and function. She made several trips to buy dividers for the drawers and other useful items, and helped me evaluate what I had and discard things that were old, worn, or out of style.

In Year Three, Sally helped me donate and distribute the furniture and larger items I described earlier. It did my heart good to know that others would be making use of the old oak pieces Howard and I had so lovingly refurbished. I knew he'd be glad of it as well.

And finally, in Year Four, Sally brought her organizing skills to bear on whatever still needed to be cleared away or repurposed. The main thing she contributed throughout her visits, though, was her love and understanding. It wasn't just the closets Sally was cleaning out, but all of my emotional baggage as well.

When I did some inquiring among my group of widows, I discovered that I was not the only one whose friends had offered up their organizing skills. **Paulina** shared a closet story with me that I think is every bit as transformational as my experiences with Sally.

When Paulina found herself facing the "closet task," two people came to her aid: her twin sister, Barbara, and her cousin Rosie. The first thing the three of them tackled was Paulina's wife Teri's shoes, which were as valuable as they were beautiful, many from famous designers. As it happened, Paulina knew a teacher who wore the same size shoe Teri had. It was an easy decision to give this hardworking woman Teri's shoes. When she later ran into that teacher at a social event, she immediately noticed Teri's shoes on her feet; nothing could have made her happier.

A lot of Teri's clothes went to Goodwill, but Paulina found that she was not yet ready to donate or dispose of the hanging clothes. "I just had to wait to take that step—to get rid of the things Teri wore every day," she shared. "I think it's important to take each step in the process deliberately, in its own time."

Today, a little more than three years since Teri's death, Paulina is finally ready to deal with the remainder of Teri's things—even the sneakers with the socks still in them and her two favorite blouses. "The only way I can describe it is that I feel the energy inside me starting to change," she said.

I call this *moving forward!*

Of all the generous souls in my life who've helped me with my process, my friend April just may have been the most selfless. Even as her own husband recovered from esophageal cancer and her daughter faced the challenges of single motherhood, April offered me her precious time and attention. Several months after Howie died, she insisted on helping me put my house in order—including the paperwork I knew I had to take care of for my daughter's sake.

April understood that this wasn't just a random goal I'd set for myself; it was part of my healing process. So one Saturday, she came from her home, an hour away, to help me go through closets and papers and accompany me on various pressing errands. Every Saturday for the next six years, she did the very same thing. April sat on the floor with me for hours, figuring out which papers I needed to keep and which I could discard. She climbed a ladder numerous times to fetch forty-seven years' worth of stuff, and then helped me decide what to do with it. She struggled with me through computer issues and router battery changes, taught me how to trim plants that were obscuring my outdoor lights, and did so many other things over those many Saturdays. There were just a few breaks in April's weekly visits, and all three of them were because she had to have orthopedic surgery of one kind or another.

April listened to me, observed my transition from weakness to strength, and understood the essence of gratitude I developed for absolutely everyone and everything. Now *that* is a friend.

I want to move on to a couple of neighborhood friends, Helaine and Gayle, each of whom has known me since I first moved to Florida more than forty years ago. They happen to travel in different social circles and only know each other from the local community, but both have become precious to me and were endlessly supportive throughout my early widowhood.

About three months after Howard died, Helaine called me and asked if I would like to begin to exercise, something we had done together decades before but had fallen out of the habit of doing as our lives took us in different directions. I had no real interest in learning yoga—the activity Helaine had suggested—but my daughter, who was with me when I took Helaine's call, said, "Mom, this is a good idea. Why don't you try it out?"

Thus encouraged, off I went with Helaine to a Tuesday-evening yoga class. We figured we might be the only two people ever to have to repeat the beginners class, but we accepted that and pressed on. Sometimes one or the other of us would have a conflict, but we both attended as often as we could.

Helaine continues to invite me to share various activities with her—a movie, a lunch, a visit to the nearby botanical gardens—but yoga remains at the center of our agenda. We've gotten better at it, and more important than that, the ongoing experience has taught me that pursuing some level of physical fitness is essential to moving forward as a whole individual. It turns out that those yoga classes have served me in more than one way: the commitment to attend class every week has gotten me out of the house and socializing (and has made the weeks speed by a little faster), and the yoga itself has made me feel better and stronger, both inside and out.

Gayle checked in with me around the same time Helaine did, and asked if I would like to set up a regular dinner with her on Thursday evenings. I so appreciated the invitation and said yes right away; my only condition was that we go to places where I wasn't likely to run into anyone I knew. So few people had been aware of Howard's illness and death, and I couldn't bear the thought of encountering someone who would ask me breezily, "How's Howie?" After half a century of being part of a couple, I was not yet prepared to announce my new status.

Gayle found us lots of places "off the beaten track," and we shared many good meals and great conversations. Eventually, we did start visiting places closer to home, though to this day, I look around, wondering whom I might run into.

Those initial meals with Gayle fed more than my body; they were something to look forward to and enjoy, and they made me feel seen and cared about. And, conversely, the socializing I did with her—as well as with Helaine—made me appreciate my alone time more. Weekends, when most people I knew were occupied with their spouses and families, became a peaceful and welcome respite for me, when I could exercise, do some work, take care of the house, or just lie back comfortably and reflect on things.

At the same time that Helaine and Gayle were beginning to urge me forward, another neighbor—Georgette—asked me over for some Cuban coffee. I had never really spoken to her, and came to find this blossoming friendship a welcome bonus. Weekly coffee dates turned into Wednesday-night dinners, and thus my week-nights began to fill up, and my life, take on a kind of structure. I looked forward to Tuesdays for yoga, Wednesdays for home-cooked meals with Georgette, and Thursdays for dinners out with Gayle. These activities moved my week along and provided me with camaraderie and fun. My new life was taking shape over time, thanks in large part to the goodness of the people around me—each of whom was giving up something else in order to spend time with me.

Three people traveled to see Howard during his illness—two of them monthly, by air. Lorraine came from New York, and Dennis came from Los Angeles. The third person, Father Pat, lived locally but was frequently out of the country. Imagine my gratitude when all three of them continued to be supportive by visiting with me after Howard died and, later on, called from wherever they were. Knowing that I could look forward to regular conversations about Howard with those who knew and loved him brought me immeasurable comfort.

Lorraine had been part of our lives for twenty years, and had traveled with us around her homeland of Australia several times over the years. During the period in which Howard got sick, she was spending six months at a time in the US, and came to see him monthly. She laughed with him, cooked him special meals, and the two of them engaged in private conversations I wouldn't have dreamed of asking either of them about. They were their own team, and I appreciated it. Since Howie's death, Lorraine and I have become our own kind of team, and have begun to travel together. I'm sure this would please Howie immensely.

Dennis had gone through his residency and the early phase of his career with Howard. When Howard got sick, we'd known him for over four decades. After the diagnosis, Dennis thought nothing of hopping on a transcontinental flight once a month to see his old friend, and has visited me several times since Howard died. He calls every other week to check on me, and never fails to inspire a laugh about the fun times we had and a sigh about the sad or hard times. The subject of Howard and his precious ice cream always brings forth a shared chuckle of fond recognition.

Howard had always suffered from high cholesterol, and I had made a point of preparing very healthy meals and keeping few sweets in the house. During his last four months, a friend brought him a quart of Butter Pecan ice cream, which he really enjoyed. This rekindled his fondness for the creamy confection, and he began to eat several quarts of ice cream a day—in bed, as he could no longer move around very much. Once, when Dennis was visiting, Howard polished off one quart of his favorite flavor of the moment and asked for another. I explained that this was not good for him and I had no intention of bringing him any more at present.

At this point, my sweet and loving husband narrowed his eyes and shouted, "Are you crazy?! I am dying of cancer. I can barely walk. I don't want healthy meals; I want ICE CREAM! What are you afraid of? That I'll DIE OF HIGH CHOLESTEROL?"

What could we three do but laugh? And, of course, I scurried off to bring Howard a refill.

Father Pat visited every week throughout the last few months of Howard's life. We'd known him for more than thirty years, and he'd often attended dinner parties around our lovely glass dining table. While Howard could still sit comfortably, Father Pat joined the two of us at our large wooden kitchen table, then at a small gaming table, and eventually at my desk in the bedroom while Howard ate in bed. Near the end, Father Pat lay in bed next to Howard, feeding him.

Father Pat and I continue to meet every few weeks over coffee, catching up and sharing stories about life with and without Howard.

Two workplace colleagues—Sheila, my assistant for almost three decades, and Jay, a fellow administrator—proved themselves great friends to me. Both were well aware of Howard's illness and its progress. They helped me accomplish what I had to at work during the most trying of times, and it was really thanks to them that I wasn't forced to take a leave or simply quit a job I loved. I can't imagine what my life would be like now if I'd done that.

And finally, there are two people who have spent the last six years calling every few weeks to check on me. Anu, a colleague, lives in Cincinnati, Ohio, and has been a wonderful friend for some thirty years. Jordan, the son of Howard's aforementioned buddy Dennis, is in California. Both have followed my journey closely, offering me support and advice about this book among many other things. Their thoughts about the importance of moving forward have proven inspirational as I have done exactly that.

All of the dear friends I have taken the time to write about here share one very important thing in common, and I treasure them for it: none has any intention of letting Howard go, and I am the fortunate beneficiary of their commitment to him. Having experienced all of this love from our friends, I am now much more conscious of being a good friend to others in need, especially those embarking on life without their mate. Also, if it is true that in order to have good friends, one must *be* a good friend, then perhaps I have done a few things right over the years.

CHAPTER FIVE

FRIENDS, LOVERS, AND FAMILY

How wonderful it is that nobody need wait a single moment before starting to improve the world."

—Anne Frank

Maybe it is an artifact of my generation, but I came of age hearing the truism that men and women cannot be friends; hormones get in the way. To disagree with this was to inspire that "yeah, right" look. But I've found that widowhood brings a new component to the issue. What I have discovered is that there is being *lonely* (which I am not), being *alone* (which I am never), and being *by oneself* (which I absolutely am and may remain so). These distinctions are extremely liberating, and I have discovered that they cut across gender lines. There are men out there who are also by themselves and wish to have friends, just as I do. What they do regarding their libido or testosterone is none of my business, and it isn't a reason to get in the way of a potential friendship.

Bud, a man I met after Howard died, reintroduced me to the theater, museums, and fine restaurants, which I thought I'd never be able to enjoy in quite the same way again. He brought me back to a life close to the one I'd lived with Howard—closer than I'd believed possible—and for that, I am eternally grateful.

Another gentleman, Scott, with whom I have become friends, loves to chat about Costco, home ownership, and past relationships—and he enjoys a good cup of coffee as much as I do. Friendship with him is not only possible but also a gift.

Sensual pleasures are not to be underestimated, but there are so many joys attendant to friendship that have nothing to do with the flesh. Deep friendships based on mutual interest, shared values, generosity, and kindness can be as durable and fulfilling as romantic relationships—if not more so. It is your privilege to decide what kinds of relationships you want to nurture throughout your widowhood, but I'd advise you not to rule out male friendships, even if you aren't interested in sharing your body and soul with another man.

About two years after Howard died, I had an experience with Bud that changed my world view significantly. I mentioned this in Chapter 1, but it's worth explaining here. Bud was listening to me rant one evening over dinner about all of the well-meaning but presumptuous friends who kept suggesting that it might be time for me to "move on." In response, he said gently, "Perhaps it is a matter of semantics. There's no reason you have to *move on*, but maybe you could *move forward?*"

His statement was a simple one, but I was gobsmacked. This idea literally changed me. I have to wonder where I'd be in my progress if I hadn't accepted Bud's invitation, as a friend, to join him for dinner at a lovely French restaurant. I certainly wouldn't have written this book.

There are kind, thoughtful, and chivalrous men out there who have their own full lives but who are as hungry as you are for connection. If you open your eyes and mind to them—and remain honest and clear about your needs and expectations, you just might find a few new people to walk beside you on your path through this phase of life.

Additionally, you might find colleagues at work who, during critical times, demonstrate their friendship above and beyond the call of duty. In my case, one such man was Nelson Soto, who has a very good soul. When I returned to work after Howard died, Nelson made sure I ate lunch, defended my decisions, and knew when to step back slowly as I grew stronger. He will always have a place in my life and in my heart.

Whether at work or in the neighborhood, people show up. Those who truly have our best interests at heart bring us gifts we can process at our leisure. They know what we need to hear and when we need silence. And if we are lucky, they accompany us along our uncharted path for as long as we need them.

That covers friendship, but, of course, many widows do find themselves moving into significant new relationships. Five of the thirteen women I interviewed developed new partnerships after a few years. Others made a conscious choice not to do so.

Lorraine's experience was echoed by a few others. She spent a number of years being friends with someone, and then, when the time was right, the friendship developed into a relationship. Or maybe it had been moving in that direction the whole time, but at its own pace. The two chose not to marry, but their relationship remains strong and continues to grow in new directions.

Sara befriended the man who would become her partner six years after her husband died. Like her, Jean-Marie was alone and needed someone to talk to. Their relationship developed naturally, though it was not without ups and downs. Eventually, Sara felt comfortable introducing him to her children and committing to a conjoined life.

"Looking back on it," she said, I can see that opening up my heart to Jean-Marie was part of a natural process. As much as I missed my husband, I realized I wanted to share my life with someone—have meaningful conversations or just go to the movies and talk about it afterward. After six years by myself, I guess I was ready to recognize the right person when he came along."

On a practical level, they agreed that he should keep his house so that if anything were to happen to her, he would have an emotionally comforting place to go back to. Blending two lives at a certain point in life is quite different from starting out together at age twenty, and often different accommodations are called for.

Rosalyn—the youngest of my cohorts, at age thirty-eight—has been a widow for three years. She expressed to me her desire for male friendship. "I think a simple evening out with a man would be so comforting," she said, "I think it would make me feel protected in a way that I don't on my own or with women friends. I wouldn't feel like I had to rush to my car after dinner, looking over my shoulder. I really miss the companionship of a man but also that sense of safety."

Margaret kept friendly company with a man for five years before he became her partner. When I asked her about him, she shared that John was very different from her late husband, Mike. "Mike was kind of an introvert," she said, "but John is very outgoing and loves to socialize. The thing is, I'm really different from John's former wife too—so I guess maybe we both needed a different kind of person this time. Maybe we *are* different from the people we used to be. When we figured that out, we kind of laughed about it."

As I mentioned, several of the women I spoke with expressed no inclination to develop a new relationship. **Netti** feels she could never give 100 percent of herself to anyone new, so she doesn't feel it would be fair to remarry. "I loved having a soul mate, walking the path with someone, being intimate," she told me wistfully. "It wasn't about being *married* per se; it was about being committed. That's what I loved about it. Even when we disagreed about important things, neither of us ever considered getting out of our marriage; we both always looked for ways to stay in it."

Netti went on to observe that many independent women—those with careers or simply financial independence—do not see a need to remarry. "They tend to be comfortable with themselves," she explained, "and don't want to turn their back on the partner they had. I really do think that Wilbur continues to walk with me and that I don't need anyone to take his place."

SINGLE MOMENTS OF SUPPORT

Support doesn't have to be ongoing; it can be a one-time thing and still have impact. A single comment or action, conscious or unknowing, might be the thing that propels you forward. In my case, two of my granddaughters, aged six and seven at the time, each unwittingly did something that affected me deeply.

A few weeks after Howard died, I returned to my daughter's house—a safe space for me.

As I walked through the front door, seven-year-old Carli came up to me quietly and said, "OK, Safta, let me take your bag. I am your new roomie, so you won't be alone! Whenever you come here, we'll sleep together!"

I thought I would faint. Years later, she is still my "roomie."

Three days after that lovely little bombshell, as my daughter and I sat outside sipping coffee, Carli's younger sister, Madison, came outside all dressed in black: short black dress, black cowgirl boots and hat, and an adult-sized black pocketbook.

"See, Safta?" she said. "I am wearing black, just like you, so you won't feel bad. It will help us both think of Saba!"

Again, I felt a little faint at the sweetness of the gesture. Both of my grandchildren understood that I felt alone, and they didn't want me to. And in those moments, I realized that I *wasn't* alone. They had filled my heart and supported me in a way that only they could.

About two months later, Madison provided another moment of support when she cajoled me into going on an outing with her and her mom to the mall, where they intended to pick out a gift for one of her friends.

"You can stay in the car if you want to, Safta," she said. "Or you can come in with Mommy and me."

"I think I'll come in," I told her, figuring that if I became overwhelmed, I would return to the car.

Madison held my hand as we walked slowly through a department store. When we got to the shoe department, a saleswoman approached us and told us about a sale on sneakers. *Hmm,* I thought, *I could use a pair of black sneakers.*

The woman brought what I asked for and all was going well, when she said, "You know, we have these in lots of other colors. The sale price is so good. Why don't you pick out a few pairs in these other lovely shades?"

As she nattered on, the room started spinning. I had made a mistake; I wasn't ready to face this kind of conversation.

Suddenly, a shrill little voice piped up beside me.

Quite emphatically, Madison said, "My Safta has told you *three times* that she only wants the black ones. You should leave her alone, and let her pay. JUST THE BLACK ONES, PLEASE—one pair!"

Eyes wide, the saleswoman turned without a word and walked behind the counter so I could complete my transaction. Once again, a single moment of support had a big impact on my life. I wore those sneakers for three years until they finally fell apart, but the memory of that moment will never leave me.

DOGS AND THE POWER OF THEIR LOVE

"Dogs are wise. They crawl away into a quiet corner and lick their wounds and do not rejoin the world until they are whole once more."
—Agatha Christie

Not being a "dog person," I am sharing the thoughts of *other* widows on the importance of their pets in the healing process. I can certainly understand how a creature that offers unconditional love at a time of pain and loss could be hugely beneficial to the process of moving forward.

"Our dog, Sydney, was really my husband's," **Margaret** told me, "but within a few hours of Mike's death, I think we both realized he was now *my* dog. He needed to be walked and fed and tended to. On a practical level, this gave me a reason to get up, go outside, and go shopping. Besides offering the kind of affection only animals can provide, his dog, Sydney, became my responsibility—my reason to keep going."

Sharon believes that fate has played a part in her process. A short time after Dennis's death, a friend brought Sharon and her young children a puppy, figuring they needed something to focus on other than their grief. "Vickie was key to our healing as a family," she told me. "Having an animal to care for became a kind of therapy for all of us, and a focus for our love."

Sallie refers to her dogs, Charlie and Macy, every time we speak; they are her constant companions. At one point, about a year after Ted died, she decided she was ready to make the six-hour drive to her son's house—her first solo attempt. She wanted to prove to herself she could do it—but she was also grateful for the companionship and support of her two dogs on the journey. "Those guys kept me company, but it was more than that," she explained. "Somehow, they reassured me I could do it." Sallie wouldn't dream of a life without animals now, although she has grown into a fiercely independent and capable woman.

When Butch died, he left Gigi, his service dog, in **Barbara**'s care. She believes the animal's companionship has helped her make it through each day since, as she gets a great deal of comfort from Gigi. "There's nothing like having a relationship with an animal when you are in pain," she said, and her reasoning echoed that of the others. "I have to walk Gigi, make sure she's fed . . . whatever she needs. It has forced me to get out of the house and keep moving. Plus, we have a bond because we both loved Butch so much."

Anusuya, too, mentioned the way in which her dog, Lilo, has kept her grounded and given her purpose. "Lilo is great company. I so enjoy walking, bathing, and grooming him. It's just a small step, caring for an animal, but sometimes when you take care of the small stuff, the big stuff falls into place."

CHAPTER SIX

FIRSTS AND FINDING YOUR FOOTING

"I love you, but I will not sit here and *wait* for this story to change. I am going to make it change."

—Erin Morgenstern

In her book *Option B,* Sheryl Sandberg shares that just weeks after losing her husband, Dave, she was talking to a friend about a father–child activity. She had found someone to fill in for her husband so her child could attend the event. "But I want Dave!" she cried. Her friend put his arm around her and said, "Option A is not available. So let's just kick the shit out of Option B."

We widows are constantly confronted with Option B. It isn't easy, but I can tell you that it does get easier over time. A widow faces many firsts, and they are often painful. I want to share my experiences regarding a few of mine.

FIRST GUESTS FOR DINNER

About two years into my widowhood, I began to contemplate having dinner guests. This was something Howard and I had enjoyed doing for forty years, hosting everything from intimate gatherings of a few couples to large celebratory events. How was I to begin planning something I thought I might never do again? I tried to tell myself that entertaining wasn't something I had to do in order to move forward, but I knew it was part of a larger issue. I had to overcome my dread of being the "third wheel" (or fifth) at a table.

I thought long and hard about it all and decided to invite two couples on separate nights—people with whom I knew I could totally be myself without fear of judgment. I called Gayle and Jim first, then Luis and Ana. (As you'll recall, Gayle is the friend with whom I have regular Thursday-night dinners. Luis and Ana are my Portuguese friends living in Miami, with whom Howard and I traveled to Portugal.) I told each couple I was asking them to a "practice" dinner, and planned the same menu for each occasion.

Gayle and Jim came first.

When the salad and French bread had been cleared away and I was ready to serve the main course, I whispered to Gayle, "How am I doing?"

"Great," she responded, but proceeded to ask me gently for some silverware.

I'd cleared it all away—including knives and dessert forks—without thinking. I was only minimally embarrassed by this lapse; it was a practice dinner, after all! The rest of the night went well.

When it was Luis and Ana's turn, there was a hitch with the main course. It was to be served with rice, but when I opened my rice cooker, I found the contents rock solid. I'd forgotten to add liquid! I explained my mistake and brought out plenty of bread. My friends were forgiving, of course, and once again, I took solace in knowing it was a practice dinner.

Several months later, I invited each couple to return for a "real" dinner. Both went perfectly—even the lobster course, which can be tricky!

By the following year, I felt ready to increase my guest list to four, and placed myself strategically so I wouldn't have to face the empty seat at the end of the table. Again, dinner went well. I've yet to press my formal glass dining room table into service, but maybe next year I'll take that step.

FIRST LAUGH

"At the height of laughter, the universe is flung into a kaleidoscope of new possibilities."
—Jean Houston

Three years after Howard died, my friend Bud was planning a trip to Barcelona with a couple and invited me to join them. I said I'd think about it, hung up the phone, looked in the mirror, and said, "I don't think so." They were leaving in two weeks. How could I possibly consider it?

When I mentioned the invitation to my daughter, she didn't hesitate.

"Just go!" she said. "Get on the plane, and go. You can afford the ticket, Bud will take care of you, and you might even have a good time. If you don't, you can always get on a plane and come home."

I had never even met the couple, but I trusted Bud—and, as you know, I think trust is key to moving forward. After a bit more thought, I embraced the idea and said yes.

As it worked out, I had to travel to Spain and back alone. I found my way to the hotel without incident and was welcomed by warm and wonderful people. What I'd never expected—and I mean *never*—was that I'd experience a major first on Sunday, December

18, 2016. Having survived walking with my old friend and my new ones through a torrential rainstorm to a restaurant called 7 Portes, we took one look at our bedraggled, soggy selves and started laughing. My companions laughed, and I laughed right along with them. This was one of those exuberant, overpowering belly laughs, the kind I had not experienced in three years. We dried off as best we could, sat, and ordered food, laughing all the while. I continued to laugh with the others until happy tears rolled down my cheeks and my head nearly hit the table! I had not laughed—*really* laughed—in three years, but that night, the spell was broken.

That trip was extraordinary in other ways as well. I thoroughly enjoyed the museums, concerts, ballets, and food. (Oh, that food! I'll never forget the tapas, marvelous fresh fish, thick hot chocolate, and more.) And I was in wonderful company. I could not have had a better time. But what stands out above all else was that night of pure laughter to the point of tears—the first time I'd laughed in years.

Sallie recalled the first time she laughed as well—the exact moment. "I was wearing gray sweatpants and a white shirt. I watched one of the dogs pee on a coconut, thought, *How bizarre,* and began laughing—and laughing and laughing!" She agreed with me when I said, "When that laughter takes over, it's like you are *back in the world.*"

BECOMING A TRAVELER AGAIN

"You must go on adventures to find out where you belong."
—Sue Fitzmaurice

In addition to its many pleasures (and the laughter), that Barcelona trip proved to be a transformative experience for me. It gave me the courage to revisit places I had been to and enjoyed with Howard. I would have to learn to forego the romance of travel in favor of other wonderful aspects of the experience—but having done just that in Spain, I knew it was possible.

My next trip was a return to Portugal with Luis and Ana. They'd been thoughtful enough to introduce me to new towns and different experiences, but some places had to be revisited: Lisbon, for starters. The beauty of that city, its unbelievably delicious food, and its unique countryside were pleasures enough to make me feel safe and happy there with my friends, though, of course, I missed Howard's presence enormously.

Traveling with a couple when you are accustomed to being part of one can be trying, even with generous and loving companions, like Luis and Ana. When I found myself feeling distraught about it, I had to remind myself that being able to travel was well worth the emotions my situation might stir up from time to time. I would simply have to choose my companions and my itineraries carefully and focus on the beauty and wonder of the places I was privileged enough to visit.

Ana and Luis proved to be the perfect couple with whom to take the leap to travel again.

Ana later shared her thoughts about creating this new experience with me: "Your decision to travel back to Portugal with us a few years after Howard's passing impressed upon us the importance of making this a memorable and safe trip—one that would not infringe on the memories you and Howard built on our prior trips. We wanted to create new memories for you—for *Arlene*. We avoided repeating day trips and longer stays in places we'd previously visited with the both of you, and focused exclusively on new experiences. Throughout our travels, we could tell you were at peace and able to enjoy yourself while honoring your never-to-be-broken connection to Howard."

How fortunate I was to have had Ana and Luis helping me reenter the glorious world of travel I'd always valued so much.

It may have taken me four years to travel without Howard, but for **Sallie**, traveling with other couples was not a challenge. "I traveled soon and often after Ted died," she said. "I ventured to New York City, Ireland, Switzerland, and other places, as I had the company of good and trustworthy friends."

Kelly, too, took off to visit far-flung friends within the first few months after George died. She explained that "supporters came from a variety of phases in my life. Some had known me since I was eight; others, I'd met in my twenties. As they lived in different parts of the country, and some of them came to me in the immediate aftermath of George's death, these faraway friends provided me the opportunity to try out traveling after his death."

I believe we are all different in how and when we take these steps. The important thing is to trust your instincts, summon up a bit of bravery, and take them.

I had the opportunity to revisit Australia and stay at the home of my longtime friend Lorraine. Again, I went to some new cities, as well as some that Howard and I had enjoyed. I even stayed in the same house at one point and dined at some of the same cafés. The key to it was that I was with someone with whom I was completely comfortable, a person with the kindest heart and largest soul imaginable. One of the things I've learned along my widowhood journey is that our trusted friends liberate us—and that is the best gift anyone can give.

Howard and I had been accustomed to spending two weeks each year in Dillon, Colorado, at a vacation home owned and generously shared by Howard's brother and his wife. We had very much enjoyed the snowy landscape and picturesque mountains in winter and the wildflowers in summer as we strolled hand in hand, hiked, and listened to music outdoors.

Needless to say, going back without him presented challenges. I very much wanted to enjoy the places where nature and romance had intertwined for us—but I found myself longing for Howard and feeling sorry for myself. How fortunate, then, to have my loving family with me. I was able to share my pain and indulge in the sweetness of remembering my husband alongside others who also loved him. Learning to accept the bitter with the sweet is just another step on the journey, one very much worth taking.

My trip to New York was perhaps the hardest for me, as it is where Howard and I had started our lives as a grown-up couple. Throughout our college years—in spite of the fact that we had no money to speak of—we'd enjoyed all the city had to offer. It was the sixties, and we'd wandered the streets of Greenwich Village and the East Village, studied at the Forty-Second Street Library (the scene of our first and worst date), and gotten engaged while being ferried around Central Park by a drunken carriage driver.

There would be no easy way to go back to New York without the "boy from Brooklyn," so I decided on the best plan I could think of: I would take my granddaughters. Carli, Madison, and I made the trip, and for the first time ever, I saw the city through the eyes of children. We visited the Central Park Zoo, went to a couple of kid-friendly Broadway shows, and filled our tummies at the M&M's candy store. It was wonderful, but . . . it was *hard*. Even my delightful and delighted traveling companions couldn't lighten my heavy heart as I yearned for my beloved Howard.

It would be four years before I'd attempt that trip again—but I did it. It's important to me (and would be important to my husband) to overcome nostalgia and create new memories to keep beside the old ones.

The last travel experience I want to talk about involves what many believe to be the most romantic place on earth: Paris. If you have never had the pleasure of visiting the "City of Light," I can tell you, it is all they say it is: romantic cafés, beautiful light, marvelous art . . . especially when experiencing it with your true love.

After he became ill, Howard lamented the fact that we hadn't managed one more trip to Paris. In fact, he couldn't stop talking about it. Sensing how important it was to him, I worked hard to come up with a way we could enjoy Paris once again in spite of the challenges his medical condition presented.

We took it slowly. When something uncomfortable happened, we laughed about it. I let Howard sleep until noon every day, and then we took a leisurely stroll to a café, where we enjoyed croissants and the finest, most aromatic coffee. We dined each night at our corner bistro and turned in unfashionably early. We might not have covered as much ground as we had when he was well, but I can honestly tell you that it was the most beautiful trip ever! Which is why going back was hard—but not impossible.

I'm proud to say that I have been back to Paris once, this time with a friend who was seeing it for the first time. Viewing that magical place through her eyes helped me to brush the tears from mine. And the coffee was as marvelous as ever.

When they say, "Travel broadens the mind," I don't think they are referring specifically to widows—but the maxim certainly applies. As painful as my trips have been since losing Howard, I am proud of having made them. The effort provided another way for me to move forward. Moving through the world is still a bittersweet experience, but I have reclaimed an activity I love.

PART II
THE YELLOW BRICK ROAD DOES NOT END IN OZ

IN THE BOOK *The Wizard of Oz,* Dorothy believed that her process of following the Yellow Brick Road in order to return home would be completed when she reached its end and found the Wizard. She believed there was a solution to her problem, and he would be the one to solve it. As it turned out, this wasn't the case. It had always been within her power to solve her own problem—reaching her destination—if only she'd known it. She was already making her journey home, through the challenges of Oz, simply by putting one foot in front of the other.

When I conceived this book, my plan was to move from the past into the present and, ultimately, the future. What I have learned is that there is no clear dividing line among these things; they are simply part of an ongoing process. There is not one single moment when the past is the past. Rather, it stays with us as we move forward. My life's journey continues step by step and the process—which began even before Howie died, as I have explained—isn't what I thought it was.

My husband passed the torch to me, and I had no choice but to accept it and carry it forward. Looking back, I feel nothing but absolute gratitude for that gift, and many of the widows I spoke with echoed that sentiment.

As I've described it, my process has been an organized one, with annual goals. The journeys of some of the other widows I spoke with have been faith based. Still other women tended to face challenges ad hoc, as they arose. Some were guided by deep cultural norms, and many found courage in the need to be strong for their children. Whatever form it takes, the widow's journey is one we don't opt into and can't opt out of, but I have found strength and comfort in hearing about the various roads we all take through Oz on our way home.

CHAPTER SEVEN

THE PROCESS IS A CONTINUOUS JOURNEY

**"You are never stronger than when you
land on the other side of despair."**

—Zadie Smith

Although it is reassuring to believe in maxims such as, "Time heals all wounds" and "Slowly but surely wins the race," it's important to understand that these statements aren't true for everyone. Many of us get stuck inside our grief, and it feels as if time has left us behind. We know we still have "things to do," as Howard told me, but turmoil and fear keep us from sensing any progress along our path. Make no mistake, though; we are *always* moving forward, however slowly. It's just that how we do it—and at what rate of speed—is unique to each of us.

My process of moving forward involved a rather practical approach. But then, I am a rather practical girl. Thus, my journey has remained a bit more earthbound than that of several of the other women with whom I spoke. It began with the successive tasks I took on in and around my house. With each passing year and each goal accomplished, I became more focused, disciplined, and capable. These qualities—and my burgeoning admiration for all that Howard had done to enhance our life—propelled me from one year into the next. As I progressed, my journey went more smoothly.

Throughout their journeys, each of the widows followed her own path forward. **Margaret, Sallie, Lorraine,** and **Sharon** each told me that their faith played a significant role in their processing of their grief. **Kelly, Anusuya (Anu),** and **Barbara** referred specifically to the significance for them of Buddhist philosophy. Kelly explained that Buddhist philosophy teaches that what is coming will come regardless of any plan, and that probably, it will be good. "I found it comforting to know that my reality was in front of me regardless of what I might do, and that I'd just have to face it," she said. "I found myself confident that I'd be able to deal with whatever life presented."

Anu made similar observations, and Barbara added that she began practicing Tai Chi breathing, a discipline engaged in by many Buddhists, to help her through her process.

Both **Netti** and **Donna** insisted that they did not have a process; they just did what needed to be done at any given moment. "It isn't that I didn't have goals," Netti explained. "There always seemed to be a list of things to do, but there wasn't a specific time frame." Netti continues to add items to her list even now, and tackles them in her own time.

Donna chalks up her lack of a "plan" to the fact that Ray was ill for so long before he passed away. "I guess it isn't so much that I was winging it as that I'd started taking care of so much of our life while Ray was still here. After he died, I just kept on keeping on."

Rosalyn, who was widowed young and with small children, echoed that her process began long before Ril died—but she sees it more as an emotional journey than a series of accomplishments. "Losing a spouse is a journey you walk alone," she told me. "My process was all about learning how to do that—shifting my identity from the 'happily ever after' fairy tale to the solo reality. At first I thought, *God, what was it all for—all that hard work we did to build that life?* But gradually, I figured out that there was no point in dwelling on it. I had to keep living and create meaning for myself. So I slogged through the muck for three years—first, just surviving and then, finally, in Year Three, figuring out that I wanted—*needed*, really—to come up with a way to help others."

Margaret believes her process began with Mike's diagnosis, which came on Valentine's Day 2003. "I began to grieve in that moment," she admitted, "and part of it was just knowing that I'd still be alive, but my marriage had no future. We wouldn't be growing old together. My former dream of growing old with Mike wasn't going to come true, so I'd have to come up with a new one."

Her words resonated mightily with me, and brought to mind the feelings I'd had early in Howard's illness. Yes, I was embarking on a process, but all I knew at the time was that I was spending many nights sleepless and tearful, knowing I'd have to get up the next morning and do what was in front of me. In Margaret's case, in addition to taking care of Mike, she had to take care of preparations for her son's impending wedding. Similarly, **Lorraine** found herself planning her daughter's wedding just six weeks after John perished in an accident, and **Anusuya** had to face her son's wedding just five days after she became a widow.

Anusuya may have been the most fortunate of the three of them, in that she had a strong framework of tradition to fall back on. Both her mother and mother-in-law lived with her, and she took her cues from them. Her late husband's mother told her in no uncertain terms that it was important for young people to marry, and that her son would have wanted the wedding to go on. With that, Anu put her mourning aside temporarily and went into action. "Once the wedding was done," she said, "there were so many other things to take care of. Gautam had already made me the cosignatory on many documents and taught me how to do many things, but I had to pick up where he'd left off. And there was also the matter of caring for my mother and mother-in-law. I had to be strong for them, so I somehow found the strength I needed."

One day just recently, I lay in bed reflecting upon all that I had been through over the past seven years. It was early morning, and a torrential rain beat hard against my windows—quite a common occurrence during the long Florida summer. Feeling secure under my comforter, sipping a hot coffee, the whole process of moving forward suddenly made sense to me. I had traveled a difficult road and was still on it. Howard would never again sleep in this bed or wake up beside me and listen to the rain—but the experience of it was still awe inspiring; the comforter was still cozy; the coffee was still hot and flavorful. Life wasn't what it had been, but it was a good life. This realization, I knew, meant that I was moving forward.

Sara told me that in order to move forward, she'd felt she needed a challenge—something she could accomplish on her own in order to establish her new identity. "A few months after Michel's death, I decided to leave my home in France and come to the United States with my kids to continue my education," she said. "After a year and a half, I got my MBA, and we went back home. Our time in the States was a kind of bridge for us; it kept us moving forward and becoming who we needed to be."

Margaret, too, began a master's degree program soon after Mike died, and reported it to be helpful to her process. "I was in a cohort group," she explained, "which involved attending some residencies where we all shared a suite. For one of them, I stayed with a friend and two other women who were young enough to be my daughters. I'd been out of academia so long, I didn't totally get how everything worked. At one point, we were told to place our writing assignments in a 'drop box,' and I asked the younger women where it was located! They patiently explained the ins and outs of cloud storage to me, and that there wasn't a physical box anywhere. Believe it or not, it was at that moment that I realized I had done the right thing. Going back to school was helping me redefine myself and get on with my life."

Sensing that Margaret might need some friendly encouragement, Margaret's daughter, Marissa, told her that if she completed the coursework for her degree within the minimum time frame of two years and one month, she would take her on a trip. It must have been just the prod Margaret needed; she redoubled her efforts and completed everything on time. She and Marissa took off for New York City, saw the sights, attended a performance of *Hair* on Broadway, and had a wonderful time.

Margaret shared another experience that touched me. "I was collecting pictures for a photo display at my son's wedding," she noted, "when I looked out the window and saw a beautiful red cardinal. He looked right at me and sort of posed until I could take his picture. Later on, when I was walking across the campus for the first time, getting ready to begin my master's program, I saw another cardinal up in a tree, watching me. Those two cardinals were like surprise reminders of Mike. It felt as if *he* were watching me. These 'surprises' caused me some pain, but also brought to life my connection to Mike. It's like the pain will always be there, but so will he."

I couldn't have expressed this combination of emotions better myself.

Lorraine shared some feelings she'd had during the first year of her widowhood. "My friends were all so kind about inviting me over for Christmas and other holidays," she noted, "but I honestly couldn't understand how anyone could be celebrating! My husband was gone; how could there be parties?! I realized I'd have to come up with some way to survive these 'joyous' times. So for the next few years, I spent Christmas Day with my children, John and Jennifer, and then packed up and went on a brief trip. It's not that I was trying to run away. In my head, I understood that life went on, and people had the right to celebrate the holidays. But it was just too painful for me at that point. It was much better for me to just remove myself from the situation." She added that the passing of time did help. Three years later, she was able to host her first Thanksgiving dinner since John's death.

Paulina reported that she could feel herself getting stronger. This past year, some three years since Teri's death—she was finally able to buy a Christmas tree and put it up, though she didn't go so far as to decorate it. "It was a step—OK, maybe a baby step—toward having a full life again," she told me. "I was giving myself permission to do things differently, and that helped me do things."

Rosalyn talked about the specific responsibilities of a widow with children. "In order to be a good parent," she said, "you are forced to live in a positive space. I wasn't a wife anymore, but I was still a mom and had to set a good example for my kids. I think that in itself helped me move forward. Ril had always believed in me so strongly; knowing that helped too."

Having been widowed twice, **Barbara** had a rather different experience with moving forward. She'd met Butch less than two years after the tragedy that took her first husband and child. In conversation with a counselor about her new friend (which is what Butch was at first), she explored whether or not she was ready to begin a new relationship. "That counselor told me something that ended up being pretty important," she shared. "She said, 'Sometimes life doesn't wait till you are ready.' While I was still thinking about it, an Indian shaman I knew suggested that I join his circle, so I did. I was instructed to put myself and something belonging to my husband and my son in the middle of the circle. The shaman then said to me, 'You were supposed to go with them that day, but you couldn't because your mission was to help another. You were left here to help others.' All of this gave me so much to think about, and, of course, I ended up being with Butch, which was the very best thing for me."

When Barbara lost Butch, who had quickly become her soul mate, moving forward involved nothing less than creating a whole new life—or at least she'd thought so. Art has become her way of "expressing anguish without screaming" as well as a way to bring something beautiful into her life. "Nowadays, I give my art away to people I think might experience the same emotional relief from it that I do," she said. "I guess I'm a bit tired of making myself over. It's just too hard. Now, I just try things, become a part of this or that group knowing that I can leave it if I want to without feeling like a failure. I know that I just have to keep looking for the right people and experiences . . . people who understand that my situation is different from theirs."

As I write this, **Anu** has experienced several other transitions. Her mother-in-law passed away about two years ago—and just a few weeks ago, her mother died. She is now without either of the women who supported her so fully when she lost Gautam. She shared with me that, like Barbara, she is tired of mourning and transition. "I am going to have to move forward in a whole new way at this point," she said. "I am not even sure what that is yet."

It has taken several years, but **Sharon** now believes that she has found her loving heart and a peaceful life. "No one can drive me off my path forward," she asserted. We then discussed some of the difficulties in her journey, such as her transition to another country (Jamaica to the US) with young children, as well as dealing with relatives who appeared to be helpful but were not, etc. She explained she grew stronger through these experiences, discovering new ways to live a new life. Sharon shared that she learned to hold on to positive things in her life while letting go of others. She then began to sing one of my favorite songs, right in the middle of a café while having lunch with me. It was a song I used to sing to myself when I needed to add humor to my choices.

Spontaneously, we began singing together that old Kenny Rogers song:

> You've got to know when to hold 'em,
> Know when to fold 'em,
> Know when to walk away,
> Know when to run.

Sharon's Jamaican accent contrasted with my New York one, causing us to laugh heartily.

Sharon offered that she had experienced some minor health issues—thankfully now resolved. Once she realized that her own health was good, she was on the road to peace of mind. Today, she focuses on her "happy space," which includes gardening, politics, and basketball. These three things, she says, keep her balanced, focused, and moving forward.

As I have come to understand, the diversity of the thirteen women quoted in these pages extends beyond culture, background, and orientation. They are diverse in how they have dealt with their widowhood. Conversing with them began as a "fact-finding mission" for me, but became much more than that: it became a part of my own process of moving forward on my own unique path.

CHAPTER EIGHT

LIFE'S LITTLE SURPRISES ALONG THE WAY: THINGS I NEVER EXPECTED

"One of the most courageous decisions you'll ever make is to finally let go of what is hurting your heart and soul."

—Brigitte Nicole

ALMOST HAPPY

Five years after Howard's death, I began to feel happiness again—within limits. I guess you could say I was "*almost* happy." The return of joy surprised me, but I knew it was real. At times, I'd catch myself singing or whistling around the house, but then something would remind me of Howard, and I'd fall back into a sad reverie. I came to understand that being *almost* happy was a balancing act that would probably continue for a very long time.

My precarious state of mind was only partly about losing Howard. Because I had moved forward in my life, I faced new challenges at work and in personal relationships, as we all do. But how was I to weigh these in relation to my grief? Would the combination of grief and worldly challenges keep me from ever being *fully* happy?

I decided that being *almost* happy might be good enough. It wasn't really so bad to dwell in a peaceful state where I was fully able to enjoy a moment, a day, an experience. So what if challenges loomed on the horizon? That is part of moving through the world—something I am proud of being able to do.

Sallie told me that there came a point when she understood that if she wanted to be happy, even *almost* happy, it was going to take work. "I had friends to do things with, but no one to do *nothing* with," she lamented—and I understood exactly what she meant. She remembers working hard at achieving some state of happiness. She came to the understanding that in order to do this, she had to take control of her life. Ted had been in her life since she was eighteen. At age sixty-seven, she began to wonder, how was she to proceed? Who was she, and what made her happy? She shared that "One night while doing the dishes, the desire for happiness just overwhelmed me. *I want to be happy again*, I decided, *no matter what it takes.*" As Ted had spent his adult life in a wheelchair, there were adventures on which they were unable to embark. She had always wanted to climb mountains and walk for miles through Ireland and Switzerland. So that was exactly what she did! These endeavors helped her create who she was to become on the path to being happy *(almost)*.

Lorraine loves the challenges involved in breaking barriers, and she knows that as long as she is alive, she has to move forward. "Rather than live in darkness, I want to come into the light," she said. "I figure, the question isn't whether I'm going to be happy or unhappy, but how will I experience each moment."

I can attest to this, and would only add that as we move from one experience to the next, we are balancing in that "*almost* happy" realm. Maybe we are even moving toward being *really, fully* happy. On our quest to find this balance, the obstacles we encounter may make life feel chaotic. I promise you, facing these things when they arise is necessary for moving forward. Although it may not feel like it, we do eventually find a measure of stability—and that is a key component of enduring happiness.

Paulina explained that as a gay widow, she believed her world to be even smaller than that of her straight counterparts. "When I was young, I could meet women at clubs," she said, "but as I get older, it is less of an option. Now, I have to work hard to find ways to develop new friendships—let alone a partnership. But I guess I'm working it out. I have this friend who has been with me through my widowhood, and she calls me 'Sorcito,' which means 'like the sun—always smiling.'"

Rosalyn related to me that four years after Ril's death, she felt herself entering into a kind of transition period, "from the 'we' to the 'me.'" As she described it, "I used to feel constantly seesawed back and forth from sad to happy, but I don't feel that anymore." In response, I shared a friend's observation about me: that I seem to have worked my way to having some "delicious moments," when the layers of sadness would lift long enough that I could dwell in the moment, completely happy and content. She was right, and I have learned to celebrate those moments.

After losing a significant other, we realize how powerful time actually is. Over time, we begin to feel more and more alive, whether we want to or not! We are forced to admit that although things have broken around us, we, ourselves, are not going to break.

NO ROLE MODEL

Before Howard died, I had little personal experience with death. None of my close friends or colleagues had lost a spouse. At age forty, I did watch my father take care of and then lose my mother over a nine-month period, but losing a parent to cancer is within the natural order of things—and my father's reaction was quite different from what mine would prove to be. Within three months, he had developed a relationship with a lovely woman named Ellie, who was kind, thoughtful, and understanding of his situation. Sadly, Ellie succumbed to cancer as well, just eighteen months later—and my father moved on to his next companion, Dot, who was neither kind nor thoughtful. Her goal was quite clear from the beginning. She took over his life, both personally and financially, and isolated him from his family. When Dot died five years later, her children inherited the home she'd forced my father to buy; they proceeded to kick him out of it.

After this, there were no more new women in his life. My brother, Martin, and I gave him attention through visits and phone calls. In spite of these efforts, Dad lived alone until he died.

Clearly, he was not a useful role model—and in any case, my response to my spouse's death was the diametric opposite of his. Unlike him, I found myself willing to be alone; in fact, I couldn't imagine anything else. When Howard's death came, it was as though I had been sitting quietly when someone wielding a machete approached me and proceeded to slice my arm cleanly off! I have rarely shared this mental image, but it was how I felt: as though a vital piece of me was taken forever in a flash.

Barbara shared that she also had no role model. She explained, "When you are the first widow among your friends and family, you become the one nobody really understands. Some people abandon you or look at you aghast, or they are there for you for a few months. You are different, and they cannot comprehend what it feels like to go home to an empty house, or that you may not want to eat. When losing your spouse, you sometimes feel like the Lone Ranger. It is often too difficult for others to grasp. Much to your amazement, you have become the role model."

SURPRISINGLY, SOME PEOPLE JUST DON'T GET IT

"You have to learn to get up from the table when love is no longer being served."
—Nina Simone

As I have explained, Howard was very private about his illness. I respected this and honored it, of course, but it did create a difficult situation for me when it came time to inform people that he was close to death or that he had died.

Two couples, in particular, were intensely angry that they had not been told about Howard's condition sooner: his brother and sister-in-law and some dear friends of forty years. Both couples lived in other states, and none of the four ever spoke to me again. Naturally, I am sad about this, but Howard's wonderful, too-short life was in my hands at the end, and I had to afford him the peace and privacy he insisted upon.

Most people we knew learned of Howard's death after the fact. Some of them were upset initially, mainly because they genuinely wished they could have supported me and said their good-byes to him. Ultimately, though, they all understood that I'd been following Howard's wishes and forgave me.

When I looked into the matter, I learned that my experience was far from unique. In a 2019 article in the *New York Times* headlined "Making Meaning Out of Grief," journalist Jane E. Brody shared her thoughts about her own husband's wishes: "My getting on with the meaning of life after his death was what he expected of me and what I was pleased to be able to do. Respecting his wishes, and not capitulating to the expectations of outsiders who might behave differently, was my way of finding meaning in the wake of my loss."

Two of the widows in my cohort experienced dilemmas similar to mine, and both were determined to honor the wishes of their dying spouses. **Netti's** husband, Wilbur, did tell people he was ill, but made it clear to her that he didn't want anyone present at the end—only her. Like me, she wouldn't have dreamed of going against his wishes. If others did not understand, or could not accept it, Netti had to make peace with the fact that it was not her issue.

Sharon told me that it was Dennis's express wish that he be cremated and that his remains go with her wherever she went in life, even if she found a new partner. This would have been an easy request to fulfill if not for the fact that his relatives wanted him buried. What she did in the end, Sharon chose to keep private— but I know it was a difficult decision to make. Whatever she did, I hope that both she and Dennis are at peace with it. Choosing between the desires of the living and those of the dead can feel like a no-win situation. You just learn to deal with it.

SOME PEOPLE NO LONGER FIT

"At some point you have to realize that some people can stay in your heart but not in your life."
—Sandi Lynn

This may be hard to fathom when you have just experienced a loss, but you may *not* need all the friends you can get. What I am trying to say is that your life just changed profoundly, and there may be some perfectly lovely (or not so lovely) people in it who no longer fit. It is not their fault, nor is it yours. As your needs change—as *you* change—there will be some collateral loss.

The first people to let go of are those who are negative by their very nature. When you had a partner, perhaps this negativity didn't affect you so much. Perhaps you didn't even notice it. We tend to be more tolerant of our friends' quirks when we have a partner to lean on. But after a loss as profound as a spouse's death, we are already fighting against the clouds that surround us. The last thing we need is someone bringing more bad weather into our lives.

Without my even asking, five of the widows I talked to brought up the subject of eliminating negativity and the people who exude it. **Kelly** was quite clear on the matter. "Although most of the people around me were supportive and helpful," she said, "there were some who immediately started telling me what I should do—how I should live my life going forward. As well-meaning as they were, those people made me feel diminished, like a 'little woman,' incapable of taking care of myself or my house. I realized pretty quickly that I had to step away from them even though they'd been important in my life with George. Telling me that my house was just too much for me . . . that sort of thing . . . it just didn't help." (Note: Five years later, Kelly is doing quite well in managing her house and her life.)

It's no surprise that Kelly's was a story I could relate to per-fectly, and another point she made resonated particularly strongly. "It is as though a shift occurs," she noted. "As widows, we become the sole center of the concentric circles around us. And, like it or not, within that small center we now occupy, there is just no room for negativity; we just can't let it penetrate from those outer rings."

That said, I'm not suggesting that it is easy to take a broom and *whisk* people out of your life. Like everything else associated with the widow's journey, it can be hard to eliminate even the most toxic people from our lives—especially when we are coping with the biggest loss imaginable. I can report that it took me over three years to permanently separate myself from a lifelong friend whom I deemed consistently negative. It was hard because we shared a history, and my history became particularly important to me after Howard died. Not only that, but I knew this woman to be a very good soul. Nevertheless, if I were to live up to Howard's example and take good care of myself in his absence, she had to go.

Netti also advocated for the elimination of negativity. "I have no time for drama," she explained. "I think of negative people as 'energy vampires' who can suck you dry. And don't get me started on trying to 'fix' them; that just isn't possible. Sometimes you just have to bite the bullet and get yourself some new friends who provide what you need: some measure of peace."

Mary, one of my octogenarians, agreed that sometimes it is necessary to "chuck" people. "They might be lovely," she said, "but your gut just tells you to let them go and look for positive people. Pushing people away actually helped me move forward." During our final conversation, Mary reiterated this advice. "Arlene," she said firmly, "if you are with someone who is negative, or has a difficult aura, dump 'em!" She then looked me right in the eyes and said, "Also, don't become a nurse or a purse." This elegant quip took me several moments to absorb. I'd never thought about it in these terms! Mary's husband, Bruce, had been gone for nineteen years, and I respected her hard-won wisdom as well as her humor.

FLASHES

Another one of the things I did not expect is that six years after Howard's death, I *still* have flashes of fear and apprehensiveness when I must tackle a household task. People think (and I used to be one of those people) that after a few years of going it alone, it becomes easier to step up and take care of business. Well, yes and no.

The first time I had to change the battery in my doorbell, I assumed this would be a simple task. It turned out that it required a specific tool and an odd type of battery that had to be hunted down. I was overwhelmed! Eventually, I got it done, but in the process, I had to fight back powerful feelings of fear and helplessness. The good news is that these things *do* get easier.

Just the other day, I discovered the battery needed changing again. This time, I knew where to locate the proper screwdriver, and I'd stashed away a spare battery of the correct size. Without much thought, I unscrewed the cover, changed the battery, and replaced the doorbell on its mount—and then it hit me. I had a kind of flashback. The feelings of fear I'd experienced the first time came flooding back. When I thought about it, I was proud of how far I had come since those early days. I guess I can handle a few "flashbacks" every now and then; they remind me that every moment of my journey is still very present in my mind. That particular flash was fairly easily handled, but some can be downright paralyzing. There are flashes that threaten to paralyze us and keep us from thinking rationally. They can make us feel as though our feet are stuck in cement. Here's an example:

In the "before times," on our many family trips to Colorado, one of the places we liked to visit was a big conglomeration of outlet stores. Howard was not much of a shopper, so he'd bring a beach chair and something to read. He'd sit peacefully near the car, looking out at a clear lake and extraordinary mountains. After a while, I would join him with some coffee and sweets while the rest of the family finished making their purchases.

On our first trip to Colorado without Howard, we decided to go to the outlets as usual. As everyone else hurried into one store or another, I paused to stand on the bridge near where Howard would sit in his beach chair. Suddenly, I couldn't move. I couldn't breathe, swallow, or cry. In a flash, I experienced the absence of Howard so deeply that it threatened to knock me off my feet. I'm not sure how long I stood there, gripping the railing of that bridge. I know that my family finished up their shopping without me, and that we went for ice cream afterward. The last thing I remember from that afternoon is the grinning faces of my grandchildren, covered in ice cream. But the flash, the pain, and the paralysis have stayed with me as well.

AN OCCASIONAL SAD DAY

Every few months, even to this day, I wake up overwhelmingly sad. This is something I certainly didn't expect after six-and-a-half years, but having examined it, I suppose it makes perfect sense. On these particular days, I want to stay quiet and alone with my heavy heart—and that is exactly what I do. I allow my tears to fall into my coffee, and then I drift about the house, un-productive and lost in my feelings.

Around four o'clock in the afternoon, without any particular effort on my part, the heavy sadness I've been carrying simply lifts. It just fades away. The next day, I feel fine. My melancholy sets in with no warning, and it vanishes the same way.

Widowhood isn't logical. Grief isn't linear. We can be moving through our lives easily when suddenly the world seems to grind to a halt. Then, just as unexpectedly, it starts up again. A veil of sadness envelops us in darkness, and then it lifts to admit the light. I have come to accept these experiences and even welcome them. They are part of the mysterious process of moving forward.

CHAPTER NINE

IT'S NOT ABOUT ME

**"What we have once enjoyed we can never lose.
All that we love deeply becomes a part of us."**

—Helen Keller

One of my strongest beliefs from the moment we found out Howard was sick was that the experience was about Howard, not me. Some of those who have been most supportive of me have begged to differ, insisting that I was underestimating the impact his illness would have on me as well, both physically and emotionally. While these individuals meant well and have proved themselves to be extraordinary in every way, they found it difficult to understand how I knew I had to move far to the back in order to keep Howard in the front.

On his way to becoming an orthodontist, Howard took many science courses, including biology. He went on to spend years studying and interpreting X-rays. He wasn't about to stop being a doctor just because he was ill. Soon after he was diagnosed,

Howard was ordered to undergo a full-body scan. Before we went in, he told me that it was my job to watch the screen for areas that lit up, indicating that the cancer had metastasized to his bones. It turned out, my services weren't necessary; the technician left the X-ray screen within Howard's line of sight, and he could view his own bone structure. Both of us could see that his entire body was lit up like a Christmas tree. The cancer was everywhere.

"I am a dead man!" he screamed before breaking down in tears.

This is not about you, Arlene, I thought right then and there—and I proceeded to behave accordingly. The tasks at hand would have to take precedence over my own needs and feelings; Howard's welfare was the priority. My job was to take care of the man I had loved since I was seventeen years old. My way of explaining this—to myself and others—was and is to say that it *wasn't about me*—which isn't to say that I was unimportant or without needs.

Several years after that moment, about three years after Howard died, I had a conversation with my daughter about my parents. A particular story came to my mind that provided insight for both of us into where I'd first absorbed this concept of *not about me* and why it gave me strength.

My father once collapsed due to a doctor's error. During a routine needle biopsy, the doctor had punctured three organs, causing my father to be hospitalized for several weeks. My mother had been present for the terrible event, and she and I kept vigil during his recuperation.

During our daily breaks, as we walked the hospital grounds, she would rub her stomach and say, "I can tell there is something wrong with me."

"Mom," I'd respond, "we are at a hospital, surrounded by doctors. Why don't you get yourself checked out?"

"Because it's not about *me,* Arlene," she'd say. "It's about your father. We have to take care of him first."

Six months later, she finally went to the doctor, and it turned out, she had terminal cancer. She would live just nine more months. In hindsight, it seems undeniable that her response—*It's not about me*—remained with me and drove me to view my own experience with Howard in the same way. She was my mother, after all, and there is no underestimating the power of a mother's words. But I hope that I learned from her experience as well. Although Howard's illness was about Howard, I did understand that I had to take care of myself too. I suppose that's really what my children and friends were trying to express to me.

Knowledge of his illness was confined to just nine people, four of whom were our children and their spouses; the other five were people whose support I needed in order to properly take care of Howard. In general, they were all extremely understanding. They comprehended the personal challenges I encountered, such as Howard's need of a hospital bed (although he refused to use it) and his inability to drink water except through a straw and eventually with a medicine dropper. (Mind you, he'd slap my hand away when I tried to employ it.) They understood that I needed help turning him when he'd bloated terribly from water retention. And most important, they understood that I had to honor his wish for privacy and his need for the peace that only my company could give him. In the end, they supported my insistence that the situation was *all about him* for as long as he lived. After he was gone, they tried to help me understand that it was now all about me.

Although I recognized how terribly tired I was and how much my eyes hurt all the time from lack of sleep (it would take me two years before I could sleep more than a few hours at a time), I knew that Howard's death didn't actually stop my life—but it did change it profoundly. Much of this book has been devoted to those changes and to the way my life has gradually become my own. I had put everything on hold for the duration of Howard's illness, but afterward, I had no choice but to reshape my world without him in it. It hadn't been about me . . . but now *I* was all I had.

"Don't feel bad for me," I would tell people. "Howie is the one who is not with us." Again, I think they had trouble understanding this. It was natural to them—logical—to feel sorry for the widow. But I could still have coffee or a glass of wine with a friend, go to a museum or a concert—enjoy life. Howard could no longer do any of these things, and I wanted my friends to understand this and reserve their sympathy for *him*.

I came to understand that I had to create a life, but what I didn't realize was that I was already living it. I had made what I now call a *silent transition*. For example, I moved from taking care of Howie's physical needs to taking care of his "stuff"—which inevitably became my stuff. The distinction is an important one, at least to me. Life continued to be about him even as it moved in the direction of becoming about me. Ultimately, it was my friends who made me understand that I had, in fact, transitioned to my new life; I was living it even before I knew that I was. This change in perspective helped me enormously and brought harmony to my days. I know now that while Howie will always be with me, and we will always be an *us*, I am also on my own and a *me*.

The widows with whom I have spoken have had to confront this change in perspective too, and they have similarly moved through the many layers that widowhood entails.

Rosalyn told me that she got to the point where she didn't want to be stuck in the pain; she needed to move through it. "The grief may always be there," she noted, "but more and more, it has begun to just pop up randomly. I let that happen and then try to move through it rather than experiencing it as a constant. I guess that's sort of like your concept of being *almost* happy." I agreed with her and added that learning to move through the pain toward happiness can help us live a more whole and peaceful life.

For **Margaret**, although it has been thirteen years since Mike's death, she still finds herself taking a few steps back rather than constantly forward. "My perspective on it has changed though," she explained. "I've learned to focus on the small things and appreciate them more fully. For example, when COVID-19 hit, I was grateful that Mike didn't have to be in the hospital during this terrible time. What if we hadn't been able to hold hands as we watched old slides together? Thoughts like this have helped me advance many layers beyond sadness and loss."

Anusuya's perspective has changed in that material things are no longer as important to her. "Over the years, I have given lots of things away that might make someone else happy in ways that no longer matter to me," she said. "And the fact that I am no longer a caregiver means I can focus on taking care of myself. My solitude—my home—has become my happy space, and from there, my perspective can continue to broaden."

THE ROCKS

"Unable are the loved to die, for love is immortality."
—Emily Dickinson

For twelve years, wherever we traveled, Howard would collect a rock—just a plain old rock—as a souvenir. When we got home, he'd take a black magic marker and print the name of the place we'd visited on the rock as a way to remember the trip. Then he'd place it outside our kitchen door. We ended up with a lot of rocks. Today, as I put my key in the lock, I look to my left at those rocks. The rain has washed away most of the writing, but I always smile at the thought of the wonderful times and places associated with each.

Of necessity, my visits to his grave are less frequent now, but I have decided that going forward, each time I make the trip, I will take one of those rock souvenirs and place it near his resting place. I never anticipated that these mementos, each representing a moment in time, would move from beside my kitchen door to his gravesite, but I very much like the idea that symbols of our shared memories are near him now. Those rocks belong as much to Howard as they do to me. Unlike flowers, stones are long-lasting; they never die. My process of moving forward continues, and with it comes greater clarity. The clouds gradually dissipate, and the sun begins to shine. The rocks remain.

Even after all this time, as I begin the two-hour trip across the state to visit with him and bring him his rock, I once again consider moving Howard from his resting place in Naples to a closer cemetery in Miami—but in the end, I choose not to do it. Naples was where he'd wanted to end up, among the beautiful gardens and tranquility. It is where he deserves to be.

PART III
WELCOME TO WIDOWHOOD

"Above all, be the heroine of your life, not the victim."

—Nora Ephron

FOR SOME, BEING THOUGHT of first as a "widow" chafes. I understand that. It doesn't describe the whole of who you are; it's a label. Like it or not though, it is the way many view you now, at least at first. Losing a spouse is seen as such a radical experience, people can't help thinking about it when they see you. My advice is to embrace it.

You are not the first to grapple with the issue of being defined by your widowhood. In my hours of conversation with other widows, it became clear that our experiences are as diverse as we are—but there are also clear threads that bind us together under the label *widow*. Exploring these commonalities has been a comfort to me, and perhaps will be to you too.

The widow's journey may take a variety of forms, but they are all about moving forward through darkness and fear, and growing stronger as we go.

CHAPTER TEN

THE WIDOWS SPEAK

"My mission in life is not merely to survive, but to thrive; and to do so with some passion, some compassion, some humor, and some style."

—Maya Angelou

As I have noted, I was approaching Year Five of my widowhood when Guy, my hairdresser and trusted confidant, asked me whether I had given any thought to writing about my experiences. I replied that several others in my life had urged me to do such a thing, and, having completed most of the projects I'd set for myself since Howard's death, I was considering it.

That wasn't the end of the conversation. At my next appointment, Guy shared that he had given a great deal of thought to my potential book—and that he had two other clients in circumstances similar to mine. He offered to pave the way toward conversations with these women, figuring they'd be as interested as I was in helping women navigate their widowhood.

I assented to the introductions, and when Guy reached out to his clients, they both agreed to talk to me. After a couple of lunches, where I did most of the talking, Sallie and Kelly became the first two women in my cohort of widows. More meetings with each of them followed, during which they expounded on a wide range of subjects while I madly jotted down notes.

As word of my undertaking spread among my family members and friends, the rest of the widows followed. Four of my ultimate group of thirteen live in the Miami area, so I was able to meet with them in person. The other nine are more far-flung—including one in France and one in India—so those conversations took place mainly by phone.

And so it began!

I was by no means a professional interviewer when I started, but over time, I learned how to conduct productive conversations during which many points of connection were made. I laughed and cried along with my subjects as we discovered how much we had in common and learned from our differences. In the end, I realized that although our situations were unique, we all spoke the same language—and that in itself forged a productive and meaningful bond.

You have already met each of these remarkable women briefly and heard some of their words. (I'm only sorry I can't share their facial expressions, laughter, and spontaneous reactions as well.) What follows is a bit more wisdom from each of them—the aspects of their experiences that I found most enlightening and helpful.

SALLIE

Sallie was my first "guinea pig," and my early talks with her cemented my resolve to include a multiplicity of voices in *Moving Forward*.

Sallie had been married for forty-six years when Ted died of a fast-moving cancer. As he'd been a disabled vet (he'd lost three limbs in the Vietnam War), Sallie had been taking care of a variety of aspects of their life that I had to work hard to learn to handle after Howard died—but, as in my case, Ted had always worked for a living and managed their financial life. Following are some of Sallie's interesting thoughts and observations. I think you'll find much to relate to, as I did.

"My first step in the 'moving forward' process was to realize that I missed feeling grateful. I knew that Ted would want me to feel grateful again, so I created a 'gratitude journal,' writing every morning from a special chair. I realized I could still feel grateful for the happy marriage I'd had.

"I knew living alone would feel scary, so I wrote about it—and I tried to allow myself the time I'd need to write and think and get happier. I began to try to find out who I was beyond being Ted's wife—and to develop my own hobbies, not just keep pursuing his. It was all part of figuring out what was *mine*.

"I had to face up to the whole money thing. Ted had always taken care of the money. It was like I thought it came from a hole in the wall at the supermarket.

"I came to see my process in an odd way. It was as if I were driving a car, and everything ahead of me was gray while the sides streaming by in my peripheral vision were brightly colored. I had to just keep driving until the colors appeared in front of me—not just on the sides.

"Early on—in Year One, I guess—I discovered how I had to deal with problems. One: step away from it. Two: divest it of emotions. And three: deal with it."

In my follow-up meetings with Sallie, she shared many more useful things. One of them was the fact that the friends she felt closest to after Ted died were other widows who'd lost their husbands before she did. (This diverged from my own experience, because I was the first of my friends to be widowed.) Sallie had already helped her friends through their own losses, so they knew better what to say to her—and when not to speak at all. "They were able to keep me busy when I needed distraction and let me talk about Ted when I needed to," she explained. I confess, I envy this aspect of her experience.

Being a survivor of war, Ted had believed he would survive his illness as well. Sallie was more realistic about it. In my own case, Howard was the realistic one. It isn't that I was unaware of the facts; it's just that deep down, I couldn't allow myself to believe the inevitable. In a strange way, I still don't! To me, Howard will always be alive.

In my final meeting with Sallie, I asked her, "What now?" She thought for a bit and shared the following: "I'm healthy now, but I do wonder how long I'll be able to function as I do, independently, without a partner. I keep tackling new things, trying to find myself. Most recently, I made the six-hour drive to see my son, with just my dog for company. I'm at the point where I enjoy meeting new people, and that makes me happy. I cook for myself every night, and while I was doing the dishes last night, all of a sudden, I stopped and said out loud, 'I think I'm happy.'" (I can relate to every aspect of this story, and I can vouch for the fact that these moments are hard-won.)

Sallie's parting comment was a typically positive one: "When you lose someone, like I did," she said, looking intently into my eyes, "you learn how fast things change. It really makes you appreciate each day and all of the people in your life."

KELLY

Kelly was married twice—the first time, for about a decade—then divorced for sixteen years, and then remarried for twenty-five. During that middle phase, she got a taste of self-sufficiency, which made her widowhood experience quite different from my own. On top of that, her second marriage came with three children and the attendant challenges. I knew I'd gain some new perspective from speaking with Kelly, and I did. Here are some of the noteworthy things Kelly shared with me.

"It was three years between George's initial diagnosis of prostate cancer and his death—so it was a long haul. Maybe that's one of the reasons I was eager to go back to work after he died. It gave me something else to focus on. I'd work, like, sixty hours a week—so for me, it wasn't about tackling projects around the house. I was used to paying bills too, and I taught myself to pay them online, as well as to work with our accountant and financial planner. (By contrast, it would take me an additional year to tackle these things. We all have to proceed at our own pace.)

"It's been around three years now. I was living in kind of a fog for a lot of that time, but I think I'm back to being my old self now. A lot of widows I know have used religion or spirituality to help them heal, but the only way I can describe my situation is to say that I disconnected with George's body but not his spirit."

In another meeting with Kelly, I decided to focus on her support system. Her thoughts about the people who'd been there for her were quite different from mine and those of Sallie, and I've quoted her on the subject elsewhere in this book as well.

Because she began working relatively soon, Kelly also made new friends from among her colleagues. These people made pleasant companions for evenings out, and she appreciated having people in her life who hadn't known her during the long period of George's illness. "I was glad to make some new friends," she said, "partly because I had to eliminate those who diminished me in any way—and I needed people to replace them." (We've already covered the issue of dealing with negative or toxic people at a time when you need all of the positivity you can get. Kelly was particularly clear-eyed about this aspect of the process.)

When I questioned her about the fact that so many of her supporters lived far away, she said that worked fine for her. "I'm pretty self-reliant," she explained, "and when something comes up that's challenging, I don't necessarily want someone to step in and fix it; I usually want to figure it out and take care of it myself." It was interesting to talk to someone like Kelly—quite different from me in significant ways—and to discover that her friends tended to be self-reliant women as well. They remain at a comfortable distance from her, available but never presumptuous about what she might need.

As I did with many of the others, in our last formal meeting I asked Kelly, "What now?" I have no plan," she replied. "If George's death taught me anything, it's that the plans we make don't necessarily pan out. So I guess I'm trying to stay open to whatever comes, and to have the inner resources I need to deal with it."

NETTI

Netti, my third widow, crossed my path in a most unexpected situation. I was attending my first funeral in eight years—a courageous act on my part—when a woman I worked with sat next to me. I didn't know her well, but we were both aware that we shared the experience of widowhood. "Does this ever get easier?" she whispered at one point. My response was, "You get used to it, but it is always horrible—at least, *I* think so." (It wasn't until later that I realized I was echoing a bit of wisdom offered to none other than the Queen Mother. In 1952, after the death of her husband, King George VI, she is said to have asked, "Does being a widow ever get any better?" The response was, "No it does not; you just get better at it.")

On the way out of the funeral, I asked my seat neighbor, Netti, if I might call her to participate in the project that would become this book. She was amenable to the idea, and we soon scheduled our first conversation.

Once we'd covered the basics, Netti expanded on her situation. Wilbur had just turned sixty when he died after twenty-two years of marriage. She had been planning to leave her job at the Urban League, and his diagnosis hastened that transition. They had just sixteen months together after that.

When I asked what Wilbur had done for a living, she compared him to the main character in the TV show *Sanford and Son*. He'd had a moving and delivery business, and whenever someone discarded something he considered useful, it would end up in their basement. "When he died, I had five pianos, seven TVs, three microwaves, over a thousand record albums, and a wide variety of furniture," she told me, shaking her head. "And in addition to two cars, there were two U-Haul trucks, a pickup, and an SUV!"

In a strange way, Cincinnati's misfortune turned out to be a boon to Netti. There was a terrible flood soon after Wilbur died, and the city ended up cleaning out her inundated basement. Still, she was left with a house built in 1875 with a slate roof, five chimney stacks, and a history of neglect. The whole experience was a mixed bag. "I really had no plan," she told me, "and I honestly still don't. I know losing everything in that basement was a good thing, but it felt as if a piece of Wilbur went with it."

Due to the suddenness of Wilbur's death at a relatively young age, their business affairs weren't in great order either. Other than getting a power of attorney in place, they'd made no contingency plan. Although this was a frightening moment, her survival skills took over. She recognized that decisions were originally made regarding Wilbur's insurance that would not be helpful now. That insurance was based on the fact that Netti had been the one who'd had open-heart surgery, while he'd been quite healthy. She now had to navigate the world of finance. What does not having insurance mean when you have no immediate employment? Back to work! Her education and survival skills had to take over.

An interesting experience Netti shared with me was when she came across a picture of Wilbur with his father. In it, Wilbur was looking out at the camera, and his father was looking at him. "It made me feel that somehow Wilbur is with his father now," she told me. "And that gives me great peace of mind. Although his family all share a burial plot, Wilbur wanted to be cremated. His cremains are in a monument facing his parents' graves, near a nice waterfall. It all makes me feel that Wilbur is OK. And that someday I'll join him."

On the subject of feeling alone, Netti said that wasn't a problem. "My son moved in to help when Wilbur was diagnosed, and he hasn't left. Plus, my niece comes over and helps around the house. I have five sisters and a mother all nearby, and lots of friends rallying around."

When the subject of her breast cancer arose, she said she thought the experience actually got in the way of her grieving process and deferred it. "I guess that's why I'm just now grieving, three years after he died," she explained.

In another meeting, I asked Netti whether she had an explicit process for moving forward, as some of the other women did. "No," she said, "nothing organized. I have goals and my list, but no real time frame."

I found it interesting that once Wilbur was diagnosed, he and Netti never had an explicit conversation about his illness. Throughout the fifteen months he lived after they got the news, he'd insist that he was "OK"—even when he was clearly struggling or suffering. "That was just his way," Netti said, "and I respected it."

Like a lot of professional women, Netti doesn't see herself remarrying. As she put it, "I don't want to break in another one. Relationships take time and energy, compromises, navigating disagreements. Wilbur and I had a serious, intimate relationship. We never looked for ways to break up, just stay together. I could never give someone 100 percent like that again. I loved having a soul mate, someone to walk the path with, but I guess I see that as in the past now."

She shared that her mother had died of cancer as well, so Netti had had two experiences as a caregiver. "Nobody really knows what it's like until they walk the walk," she said. "Those times definitely gave me empathy for anyone who has to go through it."

In our final talk, Netti reflected on where she is now. "I'm still in the bubble but moving forward," she said. "I'm still processing the deaths of both Wilbur and my mom. I don't really know what the end of all that will look like, but I guess I'm moving toward it." When I asked her what exactly she meant by the "bubble," she explained, "It isn't a world of make-believe; I guess it's more a world of disbelief. Those of us experiencing this kind of loss create this bubble around ourselves and get a little afraid to leave it, for fear of falling apart. So we stay inside with our anger, our food, whatever it is we're using to cushion ourselves from the 'real world.'"

MARY

Takako "Mary" was eighty-one when I met her, and had been a widow for nineteen years. She was born in Japan, became a nurse, and after she and Bruce married, she moved with him to Gothenburg, Sweden. She currently lives in the United States.

When I explained my goals to Mary—to share a range of experiences of widowhood, including my own—she told me she thought it was a wonderful project.

Although Mary has a large and supportive family, including five children—Steve, Keith, Cynthia, Laurie, and Clint—she confessed that she enjoys her private time. Her children visit, yet she has her own life, and her children live all over the world.

"After Bruce died, I continued to enjoy traveling, growing, expanding my mind, learning. I find I really enjoy going into San Francisco, sometimes by public transportation, so I can participate in the offerings of a big and exciting city."

Inevitably, our conversation turned to the subject of moving. Mary told me she'd considered the idea. "Over the years, I've looked at apartments and senior centers," she said, "but in the end, there was no place like home. For now, I like the peace, quiet, and safety of my house and life.

"From what I've heard, it takes most widows a year or two to move forward, but that hasn't been true for me. Maybe it's because Bruce developed dementia six years before he died, so I was already taking care of most of the household responsibilities. The support of others helped me as well."

When Mary and I focused on her support system, she had some interesting particulars to add to the topic: "Once Bruce developed dementia, he spent a great deal of time with the grandchildren. They were quite intuitive. They realized something was different, but thought nothing of it; they just modified their activities with him accordingly. I give credit for that to my kids, who never talk down to them. They were great about bringing the children to spend time with Bruce. My son, Steve, who was living in Niger, Africa, came home for a month each year and told me to go off and take a break, travel, get a change of scenery. This was the best kind of support I could have had. It gave me the strength I needed to keep going the rest of the year.

"The officers of the local police department proved to be extremely helpful too. There were times when Bruce would run out of the house, cross the street . . . they always treated him respectfully, brought him home, and cared.

"Once my kids had helped me find the right care facility for Bruce, the staff provided a very supportive environment. They knew he'd been a doctor, so if he approached the nurses' desk, they'd hand him his X-rays and some charts, which made him feel important. He had been quite athletic, so they provided him with running shoes and shorts and let him run through the halls—even in the middle of the night. They didn't drug him too much either—just let nature take its course. When I saw how kind the nurses were to Bruce, I felt comfortable going in maybe four or five days a week, rather than checking on him every day. I used the extra time to go to an Alzheimer's group and exchange ideas with other family members of Alzheimer's patients. I really grew to rely on and appreciate that support group."

In yet another talk, Mary told me about the various projects she took on as part of her healing process. Once Bruce was in a care facility, she took up golf—which proved a great outlet for her frustrations. "I took a lot of things out on that golf ball!" she joked. She also overcame her fear of traveling alone and began to enjoy it. "I found I could visit family, friends, go wherever and whenever I wanted," she said proudly. "I even went to Thailand! I guess I surprised myself with my own strength."

When I asked her what brought her joy in her widowhood, Mary immediately mentioned theater, concerts, and plays, and added, "I decided to become an usher. It's great, because not only do I get to see shows, but also I'm busy on weekends, when a lot of people are busy with their partners and families."

I began my final meeting with Mary with a question: "Was there some point when you felt that you had actually moved through your process and begun a new life?"

She seemed to know exactly what I was asking and answered with certainty: "When Bruce's illness had progressed to the point where he was no longer the person I married, I realized my life would never be the same; he was slowly leaving me. But I also acknowledged the positive things that happened each day. Like it or not, I was starting a new phase of life, and I intended to enjoy it.

"Bruce and I had always told each other that if something happened to one of us, the other should find someone who could make them happy. After he died, my children echoed this sentiment; they said they'd understand if I wanted to have a boyfriend. I told them I didn't feel I needed their permission! But I also realized that I'd never in my life been alone. I was determined to welcome this new state and find the joy in it—and I have.

"The time seems to go by so quickly," she said wistfully. I miss Bruce, but I mourn him privately, in my own way, and then go on with my life. I face whatever comes up, take care of it, and move on to the fun things."

Mary has lived a long time—long enough to see the patterns in life. She believes that about every twenty years, every person's life changes. "My twenty years of being a widow is almost up," she noted, "so I guess I'm about to go into a new phase. Even with everything, I think my life has been good. We all face our challenges; they're part of life. They remind us that we need to rely on our own backbone!"

SARA

I've already told you about my two wonderful trips to Portugal with Luis and Ana. On the second one, I asked Ana to read the first thirty-page draft of what would become this book—then just a highly disorganized little sheaf of pages. She kindly assented to do so, and when she'd finished, she told me that she liked the writing but that if it were to become a book-length work, it would need a better sense of flow. (I've since sought out the wisdom of a number of other readers, including a professional editor.)

Ana went on to say that the parts she liked best were the interviews. That led her to think of her cousin Sara, a widow who lived on a farm outside Paris. She'd lost her husband at a very young age and was raising her two young children, a girl and a boy, on her own. "Sara is so bright," Ana told me, "that it's no surprise she's an entrepreneur of sorts. I think you should interview her."

I agreed immediately, and Ana made the introductions. Sara would be my first widow from across the pond.

Sara was widowed at thirty-four, when her children were just seven and eight. After staying home with them for six or seven months, she made a decision: "I had to do something to prove to myself I could move forward and establish my own identity." She decided to move to the United States from France temporarily to get her MBA. It would take her just fourteen months.

"As stressful as it was," she said, "getting that degree was a big thing for me. I was so proud of the accomplishment and felt like it changed everything for us. When I completed my degree, I decided to take the children back to our farm in France—a great place to raise them—and when I did, I knew we belonged there. It was home. The beginning of our new life.

"Unfortunately," she continued, "when I returned to France, it wasn't a great time to find a job. When I interviewed, people seemed confused about why I'd even gotten the degree! After a year of job hunting, I decided to volunteer and use my skills and knowledge to help organize music and dance festivals, that kind of thing. For money, I rented out the land around the farm."

My initial conversation with Sara concluded on an interesting note. We were discussing the effect of her loss on her children, and she pointed out that, because they were so young, it had a profoundly different impact on the family than it would have if they'd been older. "When children are as young as mine were," she noted, "they form a unit with you; they experience the loss right along with you. In my case, we were a unit of three. I think older or adult children are different. They eventually return to their own lives and leave you to grieve on your own. Mine were with me for the duration. I can't say if this is better or worse; it's just what it is."

Our next talk circled back to the subject of Sara's farm. She explained that although she'd grown up in a city—Lisbon—she'd always liked country living. Returning to her farm meant returning to her comfort zone, and it had given her the foundation she needed to move forward. "There are days I wander out into the garden to 'pick my lunch'!" she noted. "I love growing my own vegetables. At this point, I honestly can't imagine living anywhere else."

When the conversation turned to her support system, Sara explained that her parents, who would be a major source of support for her, did not live in France, so she tended to rely more on friends. "My friends are there when I want to talk," she said, "not just about Michel but also about anything that's on my mind. They are really my family at this point." I told her that was true for me as well, as I think it is for many widows. She mentioned one couple in particular, with a little girl around the same age as her children. "That family was a double blessing," she noted, "for me *and* my kids."

In spite of their geographical distance, Sara's parents provided her with significant support. After the accident that took Michel's life, her mother came to France for two months. Even after she returned to America, mother and daughter continued to have long conversations by phone at least twice a week. And when Sara was in the States pursuing her master's degree, she and her daughter and son lived with her parents. Needless to say, the fact that they could provide her family with a place to stay and the kind of child-care only grandparents can give was of great benefit to all of them.

"When we moved back to France," she explained, "I made quite a few new friends; even though I don't think of myself as that social, there always seemed to be new people to meet. But I think I was a little wary of socializing with couples—at least, at first." I reassured her that this was my experience as well and that it seems like a perfectly natural response to losing a beloved spouse.

As Sara's circumstances were somewhat different from the other widows I spoke to, I wanted to focus our next conversation on issues of child-rearing after widowhood. She had many insightful things to share.

"I was always the one to be strong with the children. Michel was a painter; he tended to be softer with them. He'd share his work with them, read them stories, all of that stuff—but I was the one to do the disciplining. I guess that served me well after he was gone. Both my daughter and son really looked to me after Michel died, and they followed my lead emotionally. So the fact that I was strong probably helped them. Having a mother who falls apart with grief must be very hard, although I don't blame that mother. I don't blame anyone for being who they are. The truth is, my children are different. My daughter is stronger than her brother—more like me. But when we moved back to France, it was easier for him. You never know how kids are going to respond to change. I do know that we grew closer as a family. By the time we came back, we were all ready to build a new, real life here.

"The children are both grown up now. My daughter has her PhD in earth sciences: soils and mineralogy, and my son got his bachelor's in the States and then came home to complete his studies in architecture. I can't help feeling that they are doing so well because of the foundation we built together early on—enjoying cultural life together, but mainly just being there for one another.

"Six years after we lost Michel, it seemed safe and right to introduce the children to Jean-Marie, my new partner. I guess I was right about that, because they adjusted really well. It helped that my in-laws liked him too, and also that he had a daughter about the same age as my daughter.

"Looking back, I'm proud of my decision to keep the farmhouse—for all our sakes. It has involved a lot of work on my part, as old houses do, but the effort has definitely been worthwhile. I'm especially proud of one change I made. We all loved our time outdoors, so I wanted to bring some of the outdoors inside. I added these huge windows along one side of the house to create a kind of sunroom. It is so open that birds sometimes try to fly in! It's filled with plants, and we have always spent a lot of time there, building new memories upon our old ones."

In my last talk with Sara, I asked her two related questions: When did she realize she was ready to move forward with a new partner, and what was it like to open her heart to someone else?

After thinking about this for a minute, she said, "In the beginning, I really had no intention of meeting anyone. I mean, I had young children to deal with, and that was my first and only priority. But after a while, I did start to wonder if I *could* meet anyone—not if I *should*, but how it would even happen. Remember, this was before online dating and all of that stuff."

Jean-Marie—the man who would become Sara's partner—was actually someone she'd known when she was married. About six years after Michel died, Jean-Marie's wife left him, and the two gravitated toward each other as friends at first. "I guess we both needed someone to talk to," she explained.

Their friendship developed naturally into a relationship, but it wasn't without the typical challenges of trying to bring two families together. At first, Jean-Marie's children were hostile to Sara, concerned that she was trying to take the place of their mother. "After a while, all of that stuff calmed down," she told me. "We weathered it and learned how to make everything work."

So much for the logistics, but what about the emotional issue of opening one's heart?

"For me, it was kind of a natural process," Sara said. "As time passed, I started to feel alone. I missed meaningful conversations, going to a movie and talking about it afterward . . . all of that stuff. So when my friendship with Jean-Marie started to feel like more, I welcomed it. We had all of these common interests and thoughts; it just seemed right. But we were also realistic about it. We went in with our eyes pretty wide open. I mean, Jean-Marie didn't sell his house even after he moved in with us. When you've been through big changes, you understand that there are no guarantees of *anything*."

Among the challenging experiences Sara has had since losing Michel was a bad car accident that put her in the hospital for six months. Fortunately, she recovered—but it left her with severe double vision. She couldn't read or drive, and life became extremely difficult. For a long time, doctors told her that there was nothing they could do to help her—until she found one surgeon who said he might be able to help. In 2019 she had the surgery he'd suggested, and it was successful! She'd taken control of her situation, remained hopeful, and everything had worked out. "I honestly believe that one has to take on whatever challenge comes along and be proactive—no matter how scary it is," she said. "I'm lucky that I have the strength to do that, and also that Jean-Marie is a supportive partner to me."

LORRAINE

The first two widows I interviewed, Sallie and Kelly, lived within a half hour of my home. That made it easy—and very nice—to see them occasionally after we finished our "official" chats. At one of these breakfasts with Sallie, she mentioned a widowed friend of hers whom she thought I might be interested in talking to. This lady, an accomplished artist named Lorraine, had lost her husband in the crash of a small plane about fifteen years earlier.

I was very happy when Lorraine agreed to meet me for lunch at a quiet restaurant. After exchanging pleasantries, she jumped right into her story.

"Because my husband, John, died in a plane crash, he went off to work in the morning and never came home," she stated.

This shook me to the core. I simply couldn't imagine something so abrupt and devastating.

"I'll never forget a second of it," she continued. I was painting a mural in Pembroke Pines, about twenty-five miles from where we lived, when I got a call from my friend Wayne, John's friend for more than twenty-five years and part of his flying community. 'John has been in an accident,' he said. 'You need to go home right now. Just . . . stop painting, and go.' I tried to get more details, like what hospital he was in, but Wayne just kept saying, 'Go home.' As I got close to the house, I knew immediately that something terrible had happened. There were already people outside—photographers and . . . reporters, I guess. My first thought was that, in the middle of planning my daughter's wedding, I'd have to plan a funeral!"

We sat for a few minutes as I digested her story, but Lorraine had come prepared. "Forgive me," she said, "but I'm a pretty analytical person. To prepare for our talk, I made some notes, and came up with five main points. Would you mind if I just went down the list?"

Mind? I was awed to encounter someone who had the presence of mind to organize her thoughts around such a tragic experience. Here are the five topics Lorraine wanted to cover with me:

Her Emotional State

"Initially, I was shocked. Disbelieving. John had been perfectly healthy, so I hadn't even considered this possibility. I didn't get to say goodbye. All of this made me so despondent—like a zombie. I couldn't figure out what to do with myself. And then the fear and anxiety set in. I kept thinking, *What do I do? What do I do? I have no job, no income, no insurance.* I went on antidepressants, which helped. When people would say, 'You are strong enough to deal with this,' I couldn't bear to respond with my true feelings, which were that I was barely strong enough to pull the covers over my head, let alone live my life. Eventually, though, I started to feel safe. Thankfully, my home was restorative to me. I grew to appreciate the peace of being alone."

Her Physical Health

"At the time of the accident, I was in the middle of oral surgery; the dentist was preparing me for an implant. We stopped that, and I just got some bridgework. I was too traumatized for a big procedure. I knew that no matter how I felt, I had to take care of myself physically, but luckily, I didn't have any special needs, and there were people around me to help. I did still need fuel, in the form of food, even when I couldn't taste anything. I often had to be reminded to eat. When I skipped meals, I just felt weaker and more stressed out, so I'm grateful to my family and friends for forcing some food into me once in a while."

The Timing

"Six weeks after the accident, my daughter, Jennifer, was getting married. There was really no discussion of changing that because I knew John would want us to go forward as planned. He'd just taken the invitations to the post office because he hadn't wanted to just drop them in the mail! They arrived at people's houses the same day everyone heard the news. Originally, I'd asked my daughter if I could join her dad in walking her down the aisle, and she had said, 'No, Mom, that will be my moment with Dad.' But in the end, I was the one who walked with her. I was so nervous about it that I practiced for days and went over and over the whole thing in my mind. I wanted the whole day to be about my children, not about me and my grief."

Her Finances

"I had given a month's notice at my job because I had wanted the time to prepare for the wedding and begin other work. I never went back after John died, though I owed them a few more weeks. Of course, without him, I'd have to figure out how to afford my life on my own. It ended up taking me six months to get another job, which I desperately needed—not just for the paycheck but also for the insurance and other benefits. The day I began the new job, I cried all the way there and all the way back. One thing I started doing that was good was packing myself a big lunch every day so that when I got home, I could just snack on crackers and peanut butter. Somehow, not putting a regular dinner on the table just for myself helped me."

Her Way of Moving Forward

"Not long before he died, John had slipped on some water that had leaked onto the kitchen floor. After he picked himself up, he came into the living room, where I was sitting, and said, "What else could go wrong?" I thought about that a lot in the weeks and months after. I became extremely protective of my children, maybe because you never do know what can go wrong! I started treating them like they were teenagers, not grown-ups. But eventually, somehow, we all figured out how to relate to one another and move forward. I learned how to start treating them as adults again, and that was the beginning."

Lorraine had a lot more to say about the period following John's death. Like all of us, she had to deal with his belongings. And like all of us, she found it very difficult. "I just couldn't have any of his stuff around me," she said. "Especially the airplane stuff. He had lots of books on the subject, memorabilia, model planes, airline pens—I got rid of all of it. The airplane stuff made me mad, so I got rid of it! Maybe it sounds weird, but I started thinking of planes as John's mistress. In the end, his mistress got him. Wouldn't that make you angry?

"Then there was the issue of his clothes. I couldn't bear to remove them from the closets. Luckily, my daughter, Jennifer, was there to help. She sent me away to Orlando, and she and a friend, Judy, took care of all the clothes and personal stuff. Everything John had ever touched conjured up a memory for me, so this helped me enormously."

When I asked her about going out, Lorraine said she couldn't bear to go to any of the restaurants they'd gone to together. I told her that sounded pretty familiar—and made perfect sense. Early on, her coworkers were kind enough to change a reservation to a different restaurant for this reason—a very kind gesture toward their new colleague.

John had owned a big Dodge Ram truck; it was the vehicle he'd driven to the airport on the day he died. Not surprisingly, Lorraine didn't want it anywhere near their house. One of her friends took it home, and her kids arranged for it to be sold.

Milestones—holidays, anniversaries, special dates—are always very hard. Lorraine's way of facing them was to come up with an activity. She would go visit people or take a little weekend trip—anything to change up the routines that had been a part of her marriage.

Sheer exhaustion—both mental and physical—kept her from tackling any large projects around the house for the first six months. By the time that period had passed, she was working again. "Honestly," she said, "I didn't worry that much about the household stuff. Having a new job was good for me. I even made some single friends I could take vacations with. I loved my old friends, but most of them were married couples, so traveling with them would've just been awkward and sad."

This particular conversation concluded with Lorraine talking about her belief that we all have to "go outside ourselves to grow." She explained that she'd always been very close to God and believed he was there for her. "Even as a child," she said, "I had faith. Even the day John had the accident. I'd been painting a mural over a tub, and I tripped, but thankfully, I didn't fall. I remember very clearly thanking God for protecting me. When I looked back on it, I just knew that John had died at that very moment. What can I say? I can't be bitter because I have to be grateful. I honestly believe that having a grateful heart is healing."

The focus of our next conversation was support systems. Lorraine's main one, of course, was her family. Because of the abrupt and terrible circumstances of John's death, they rushed to her side—something for which she will always be grateful. But there were others who showed up as well.

"Right on that first day," she told me, "one by one, people just came. They brought food, coffee, anything and everything that might bring me comfort, in addition to their presence and their genuine love. One friend not only brought coffee, but also a coffee maker, because she was concerned she wouldn't know how to use mine and didn't want me to have to think about it.

"Within the next few days, two sets of cousins plus an aunt and an uncle came from Tampa. The cousins brought air beds and slept on the floor, listening to one another snore and becoming closer in the process. My mother slept on the sofa with her friend Sallie—there were people all over the house. They were just *there* for me, without asking anything of me."

A few weeks later, Sallie came over and organized Lorraine's bills. I understood why immediately, since Sallie was the widow who had known nothing about her family's finances when her husband died. She obviously understood that this could be a challenging aspect of widowhood and wanted to help. I love the idea that a widow might grow from student to teacher. I suppose my version of that was to write this book!

One form of support that Lorraine wasn't expecting came from her brother. He began to write her a check each month. When she questioned his generosity, he simply said he knew she needed it, and that was that. He continued to do this until his death nineteen years later of a massive heart attack—yet another abrupt, completely unexpected, and immeasurably painful loss. There were other monetary donations as well, which had been requested in the obituary in lieu of flowers. The money that friends generously offered helped sustain Lorraine until she found her new job.

After working for several years, Lorraine was able to retire, and she now finds herself happy to be done with offices. She loves not setting a clock or sticking to a schedule. She devotes her newfound leisure time and energy to painting and other creative endeavors and, like other widows I talked to, has found herself in situations where she can be particularly supportive of others. "On a family trip to Key Largo," she said, "we stopped at a small shop called Anthony's that sells coastal-type clothes. I started chatting with a woman who worked there, and she mentioned that she'd recently lost her husband and really liked being busy and productive. She also mentioned that she was a painter—so I really felt we had a lot in common. I found myself offering her a lot of advice about opportunities in the art world, and also about the experience of moving forward after widowhood."

Once again, the student becomes the teacher—and the beat goes on!

One notable thing that came up was the issue of decision-making as a single woman. "It can be hard to make decisions on your own," she observed, "but on the other hand, there's a lot of freedom in not being accountable to another person or having to compromise. Remember, I was married at eighteen. Running my own life took some adjustments, but I certainly see the good side of it. My happiness is in my own hands now, so I have no excuse for not seizing it, or at least trying to. I'm still figuring out who I am and what I want. It's an interesting process. It's not bad—just different."

After suffering a heart attack, Lorraine chose to volunteer for an organization focusing on women's heart health. Recognizing her skills, the group's leaders sent her to workshops at the Mayo Clinic in Minnesota. She now uses what she learned to help other women understand this important aspect of their health—particularly women of color, who are at a higher risk for heart attacks.

In my last talk with Lorraine, I wanted to understand where she felt she was at that moment and where she was going. What were her strategies for continuing to move forward? Her responses were, as always, thoughtful and constructive.

"When John was alive, his wants and needs affected what I did, of course. But he's not here now—so I have to really figure out what *my* wants and needs are and try to fulfill them. I've had to let go of some anger I had about decisions from the past, but I'm doing that. Life is unpredictable and precarious, but there is no place for hopelessness.

"I think some widows find it hard to accept that their life has changed. They get stuck in a bad space—vengeful and full of regret. I never want that to be me, so I just get out and get busy. Lately, I've been thinking about the things that really make my life special. At the top of my list are my painting and my love of learning. These things bring me happiness, but they also make me a better person. With all of this on my mind, I recently contacted two other artists I know and asked if they wanted to go to a workshop with me in Tequesta, Florida, given by a great teacher. They said yes right away—and I think, after we finish that one, we may go to an even longer workshop in Tuscany. These are the things that make me happy to get out of bed in the morning.

"My friends are always after me to read novels. I know they get a lot out of this, but I haven't really been into fiction for quite a while. When I do read something, it's usually a self-help or how-to book. I gave in and tried *Where the Crawdads Sing*, which everyone was raving about—and you know what? I didn't really enjoy it! I kept thinking that instead of reading a story dreamed up by somebody else, I should be creating something of my own. I should be making a painting or even just painting a wall! As we get older, we have to recognize who we are and be true to it. Not everyone is a fiction reader. I have to stick to what makes *me* happy, not what others choose for me.

"I definitely think I'm still growing, and no matter how long I live, I hope I always will be. If that's what you mean by 'process,' then I guess the process continues until we die. I'm so glad not to be one of those people who spend their lives complaining that life has treated them unfairly. It's so much better to find what brings us joy and focus on that."

Before we parted, Lorraine thanked me for channeling my thoughts and those of others into this book. "You're doing what you're supposed to be doing, Arlene," she said, "and I hope that your voice and all of our voices will be heard by lots of women who need to hear them."

PAULINA

Paulina came to me through my neighbor Georgette, who thought it might be beneficial for me to interview a widow who was gay. I agreed, Paulina agreed, and a breakfast meeting was organized.

Paulina and her wife, Teri, were friends first, and remained best friends over the course of their twenty-one-year marriage. Like most of us, they were confident they would grow old together, enjoying their life, but that was not to be. At the age of sixty, Teri died of cancer.

In the wake of her crushing loss, Paulina was "frozen" for a month, unable to do anything and wanting to simply disappear. After that, her suicidal thoughts ebbed, but it would take her eight more months before she could really admit that Teri was gone and plan the release of her ashes into the ocean as she'd wished.

Gradually, Paulina healed. "After about a year and two months," she told me, "I started to notice the colors we'd used throughout the house and decided to change them." (This reminded me of Sallie, widow number one, for whom it had taken a year before she noticed the colors in the world.)

As Paulina began having more contact with friends and family, she encountered those inevitable "well-wishers" who came bearing advice. Like virtually every widow I've encountered—myself included—Paulina was advised over and over that she should move out of her house. "The only thing more annoying to me than people telling me to move," she said, "was people telling me to move *on*. I knew I had to follow my own instincts, so I just smiled, thanked them for their concern, and did what I thought was best."

So, what did *moving forward* mean to Paulina? She described it as a mental and emotional healing process. "Today, I mainly feel grateful," she said, "and when I think about Teri, I dwell on our happier moments. For one thing, I no longer think about her in the wheelchair she had to use at the end. I don't see her weak and sick, but active and vital. This makes sense because we had so many great years together—two decades; why would I want to dwell on the bad parts?"

Paulina confirmed that she has reached that point of "*almost* happy" I described earlier, though she feels she has yet to figure out her purpose. Part of this, she knows, is to be present in her own life and kind to others. "I've always enjoyed my role as '*tía*'— aunt—to my nephews and nieces," she told me. "Helping them is part of my way of being happy, though my happiness is still far from complete. Maybe there's some kind of switch I can turn on in order to recover my joy, but I guess I haven't found it yet. Still . . . I'm grateful every day for the love I have now and the great love I shared with Teri. Not everyone gets to experience that.

"The death of a spouse," she continued, "creates this big reality shift; everything under your feet *moves*, and you're just hanging on. It's a very complex situation, and I'm still navigating it. In order to calm down and empty my mind, I use this meditation app on my phone. It helps me get into a meditative state so I can figure out what I'm going to do that day.

"At one point, it became clear to me that I could use help getting through the experience of loss, so I began to work with a kinesiologist—someone who has studied human movement and its impact on healing. She told me to imagine that my heart was full of light, and then to move that brightness to wherever I was feeling pain. I couldn't believe it, but it worked!

"I also sought out a spiritual advisor who helped me remain close to Teri. She reminded me that Teri will always be with me through the love we shared, but that she now must move in another direction."

As had become the norm in my interviews, my second meeting with Paulina focused on her support systems. She was quick to acknowledge the many supporters who are still in her life.

For the first month after Teri died, Paulina got many calls and offers of help, but she only felt like seeing her twin sister, Barbara, and her cousin Rosie. At that point, she felt comfortable only with family. But when she went back to work, her colleagues began to take a role in her healing process. She began to accept invitations to socialize, and slowly she was able to allow people's love and care to open her heart.

Paulina's work keeps her pretty busy. She still loves what she does, but sees it a little differently now. "Before Teri died, I was known for being pretty demanding at work," she told me. "Now, I think I am more patient and tolerant—of myself and others. If something doesn't work out, I don't have a fit; I just work on finding another solution. I want things to be easier, so they are! I just don't let the little things become overly important.

"I also find support and purpose in helping out my niece, Catie, who is in Tampa, studying architecture. Her mom—my sister Birdie—died of cancer, and now the whole family is pitching in. I go see Catie about once a month—and when I'm there, I stay with Libia, my first girlfriend. We were together for ten years, and she's my niece's godmother, so her friendship means a lot."

Paulina explained to me that as a gay woman, her world was smaller and harder to navigate than a straight woman's might be. "When I was younger and more social," she said, "going to clubs was an option for meeting friends and potential lovers. But as I got older, that wasn't what was important to me and my friends. We just wanted to come together organically and form a loving group. Friendships and partnerships arose organically from that group, and they all mean a lot to me.

"Teri and I used to go out to dinner on Thursdays and Fridays, so I needed a new plan for that. Now I try to see my sister Barbara and cousin Rosie on those nights. Sometimes I even go to happy hour somewhere by myself, just to socialize. But honestly, Sundays are the toughest. I enjoy my quiet time on weekends, but by about 1:00 p.m. on Sundays, I find I want to get out with people. So I've learned to make plans ahead of time. I accept almost all invitations, and I have found a lot of comfort in spending time with people. I know how lucky I am to have both family and old friends who support me—and now I feel I'm ready to evolve even further and to make *new* friends. I know Teri wanted me to enjoy my life and find my own place in the world—my own voice. That's what I'm trying to do."

Paulina shared with me that she is beginning to think about what she'll do when she retires. "I might even try to live in three different places," she said, "Miami, Buenos Aires, and Spain. I've always loved traveling and have learned quite a lot about the history of these places, so that's part of it, but I also have friends in all of them. Others will come to visit, I hope."

At the beginning of our third visit, I asked Paulina how she was doing. I was pleased with her response that she was moving forward "bit by bit." She chose to fill me in on her household tasks. "The storeroom has been cleaned up now," she said, "thanks to my sister. There are still a few big things left, but some friends are going to help me with those. The next step will be to tackle Teri's dressers. So many of her T-shirts were souvenirs from our trips; I can't help experiencing all these memories when I look at them. But it's time to donate them."

Paulina couldn't help smiling when she told me she could feel "something happening" to her. "Arlene, I'm getting stronger," she said. "I have energy again. I'm starting to understand—to really *feel*—that it's OK for me to want to do new things, to move on with my life. I hope what I mean is *move forward,* but I guess I'll see. As I keep telling you, I know Teri would want me to, and that does help.

"Teri took care of me in so many ways, but the fact that I have learned to take care of myself is definitely a good thing. I've moved beyond guilt and pain. I know I'm allowed to be happy or—like you said—*almost* happy. Those guilt feelings were really my biggest issue. I think it's because it tapped into the guilt I felt when I came out. Back then, my friends became my family too, so there are a lot of similarities."

I was particularly moved by a story Paulina told me about a woman in her apartment building. This woman had lost her husband when she was in her thirties. She's remarried now, quite happily, but she confessed to Paulina that she still thinks about her first husband every day. To me, this illustrates that the process of moving forward doesn't mean we don't look back. Whether we remain single or remarry, we all have to learn to do both simultaneously.

Paulina said she intends to remain in her apartment for at least another year, maybe much longer. "I honestly don't know," she said, "but I know I don't have to make that decision yet. I might retire even earlier than I'd planned; I've been working from home a few days a week, and I like it. Maybe I'll do some consulting . . . The point is, the future is pretty open."

I'd call that *moving forward.*

We started our final conversation with a bit of a recap of all that we'd previously discussed. We talked about changes to

Paulina's apartment, the things she is letting go of, and the ways she is simplifying her life.

Two friends have expressed interest in dating Paulina. When I asked her how she felt about that, she said, "I haven't really moved into that space yet, but I won't lie: it did make me feel good! I think I told you . . . Teri explicitly told me she wanted me to be with someone—that I was too young to give up on love. So, I'm not ruling it out when the time seems right and the person seems right.

"I think my feelings about everything are transforming. I'd still say I'm bereaved—that I'm experiencing grief—but it's evolving. There's a kind of acceptance I feel now. Teri is still with me, but I'm also moving forward without her. I have no need to find another Teri; I'm happy in my life. Of course I miss the companionship, but I kind of like the freedom to do what I want: go out, stay in, see people, be alone, whatever feels right. I know that Teri wants me to go on with my life, and I know that means change. Before, everything was related to our partnership. We made decisions together, took each other's feelings and opinions into consideration. Now—for better or worse—I don't have any of that. In a way, it's liberating."

These feelings of freedom have inspired in Paulina a new attitude about life. In spite of the pain and feelings of loss she has suffered, she sees no reason to become bitter or take it out on others. As she colorfully put it, "Nothing can match that shit, so you just have to move on!" The experience and her reflection on it have made her not only stronger, but also softer and kinder. "Teri's pain was so hard on her and on me," she said, "but now she is out of pain, and my life is lighter."

ROSALYN

My initial connection to Rosalyn was that we worked at the same university. When her husband died, the vice president saw how distraught she was and asked me to speak with her—which I was more than willing to do. Rosalyn was only thirty-five at the time and had two children, Matilyn and Gwendolyn, aged five and three. Her husband, Ril, had succumbed to liver disease after a long illness.

You'd think that I might have known exactly what to say to her, but the truth is, I had very little experience at the time in dealing with the grief of others. I shared some of my own experiences, hoping they might provide some perspective, but it would take Rosalyn three years before she was ready to add her thoughts to this book. After a long process, she has finally gotten to the point where she hopes that sharing her experiences might help others. Her story is an affecting one, and I think of her as a model of courage.

When we met for our first official interview, Rosalyn began by telling me about Ril. He'd been ill for about seven years before he died. They'd only been married a year when he was diagnosed as diabetic—a challenge they met together. Next, he learned he'd need a liver transplant, which he received when their first child, Matilyn, was two years old. After a few years of relatively good health, things went downhill steadily.

As hard as his death was on Rosalyn, she knew she had to put her girls, Matilyn and Gwendolyn, before her own grief. As a mental health counselor, she understood that children are deeply affected by grief, and that helping them develop resiliency would guard against ongoing trauma. She would have to be fully present for them and involved in their lives, and that meant putting her own grieving process on hold for a while. "It would have been so easy and natural to just fall apart," she told me, "but that would have been a terrible way of honoring Ril."

Changing the subject back to her own process, she said, "Ril had been sick for so long . . . I guess I really started to grieve before he died. In many ways, I was alone—but he was still there, and I wanted to cherish that. While he was in the hospital, we'd have these little 'hospital dates' where we'd rate the food and accommodations as if he were staying at a fancy resort. We'd laugh a little, chat about things . . . he actually comforted *me*. Of course, all that ended when he died. It was inevitable, and we knew it, but it changed everything. I don't think other people really understood how hard it was for me to accept it.

"It became crucial to me to surround myself with people who *could* understand my feelings, who could support my grief and not expect me to 'get over it.' There were a lot of good people, family and friends, who couldn't accompany me on my journey at that point."

When I asked Rosalyn about her time frame, she explained that throughout the first two years after Ril's death, she was simply surviving. It wasn't until the third year—the current year—that she'd decided to live a little more. "For me, this meant just going places," she explained. "The girls are getting older and have more friends. They want to socialize with them, so I realized I'd have to do the same. At one point, I bought three tickets to see *Wicked*, figuring I'd take two friends or family members with me. The funny thing was, nobody wanted to come—so I went by myself. I cried the whole way there and bought myself a glass of wine in the lobby. The show was amazing, but next to me were two empty seats. That was tough. For a while, I didn't want to go to the theater ever again . . . but then *Rent* came to town, and I really wanted to see it. This time, I only cried at intermission! Then I went to see *Hamilton* and pretended I was with the people next to me. That time, I didn't cry until I got home."

While learning how to go out, Rosalyn also had to learn how to live alone. "I realized just how much I missed having someone who wanted to see me happy," she told me. "My whole identity had to shift away from what I'd always wanted, which was to be a wife and mother, to being something else entirely. I guess I'll never totally figure that out, but I started to feel that at least, I could try to help others—which is one reason I decided to sit down with you and contribute to your book. Listen . . . I don't want to sound so self-pitying. I actually think I'm a good person, and someday my life will be good again. I might even find love again. I honestly hope so."

In our second meeting, I said I was curious about any sources of support Rosalyn might have had. She mentioned that when Ril got sick, she'd joined a "well spouse group." "They explained to me that I couldn't die with him," she said. "It may sound obvious, but I needed to hear it, and it really helped me stay among the living after he died.

"At some point, my mother told me that her father's mother had been widowed in her thirties, when she had nine children. 'She was a very mean woman,' Mom said, and I thought, *Well, of course she was!* I honestly believe that we widows have a responsibility to take care of one another. So here I am, trying to become a helpful member of the widow community.

"At the beginning," she noted, "certainly my family were my strongest supporters—my sisters, my mom, and my dad. When Ril fell to the floor and the paramedics came to take him to the hospital for the last time, my family came running. They helped me keep the girls in their rooms so they wouldn't have a lasting memory of Daddy on the floor with tubes coming out of him. Later on, after Ril died, my sister Cynthia took the lead. When I was just numb, she ran interference for me. I knew people meant well, but I just couldn't handle them. I was just a mess, gasping for air."

Eventually, Rosalyn joined an online support group for widows who had been caregivers. "That was a good move," she told me. "I needed to preserve those memories of caring for Ril, and talking about it helped me do that. But I had other needs as well, so I found a different online group—for widows with children. I'd strongly urge women to seek out an online community. It doesn't magically remove the pain—and family is still very important—but family members may not be able to understand the emotions of widowhood. Only other widows can do that. I still look for people I can have reciprocal exchanges with about my situation. When I'm struggling for balance, I say to myself that I am both a mom *and* a grieving widow. It helps to have people who can understand that.

"I also need people in my life who understand what it means to be a working professional while grieving—who understand the importance of holding on to your personal dreams in life. Ril was always so encouraging, even when he was in the hospital and I was trying to get through my PhD program. He would *not* let me stop my studies. So if I were to give up on my work now, it would be going against what Ril wanted for me. Since I don't have him to push me anymore, I have to find people who will kick me in the ass when I need it—or at least listen to me complain about my day.

"Believe it or not, my girls, Matilyn and Gwendolyn, are a kind of support system too, without even knowing it. They're watching me every single moment, which means I have to be strong. I have to model the best possible behavior for them. They've seen a lot, and sometimes we have to talk about it, which helps me process my feelings.

"Soon after Ril died, Matilyn was eager to go back to school. I knew it would be good for her, but I also worried about her feelings—so we talked about how she might deal with grief in a public place. What should she do if somebody says something that triggers her feelings of grief? What if she feels like crying at school but doesn't want to call attention to herself? 'You might have to save those feelings for later and bring them home,' I suggested. I also discussed the situation with her teacher because I knew she had to be part of Matilyn's support system. We agreed that the teacher might give Matilyn a hug and let her retreat to a quiet corner with her journal if she needed to. What I didn't anticipate was the piece of chocolate she would throw into the bargain—which never hurts!"

Rosalyn told me that within her group of friends, she has always been considered the strong one. "Some of them are married; some aren't," she told me. "Some are older than I am and have children graduating from high school. They were there for me through Ril's two transplants . . . and even further back than that. They were there during my difficult pregnancies and Gwendolyn's own medical problems. I guess they figured that if I could get through all that, I could navigate Ril's death."

Like Sara and Sharon, both of whom had young children when their husbands died, Rosalyn is fully aware that her children will eventually move on and have their own lives. "I don't ever want them to feel they have to take care of me," she said. "So it's good for them to see me socializing a little bit. Having my barber as a friend gives them a male role model too." (In Rosalyn's community, the person who cuts one's hair is called the barber, and the one who styles it is called the hairstylist.) "When I mentioned that to him, about being a role model, he was flattered and went on to suggest that the girls might enjoy classes in chess. He pointed out that most chess teachers are male—so I enrolled them, and sure enough, the girls acquired yet another male role model. And he happens to be a great guy too, who often talks about the life lessons the kids can learn from chess. I feel this was a good step for them, which means it was a good step for me."

Did she find herself taking any new steps in her process, I wondered. "Yes!" she responded immediately. "I think I've made some real moves. First of all, I could go into the parking lot where Ril's car used to be and not feel tremendous guilt about letting his car go. Believe it or not, that was a big thing. I realized I could move forward without worrying I wasn't a good wife anymore.

"Another thing is that I am learning to let go of my expectations of the people close to me. I get that people don't fully understand my feelings of sadness and weakness, and that's OK. I don't judge them for that, which leaves me free to focus on how to fill my emotional needs. I guess that's something I'm still trying to figure out."

Rosalyn was quick to point out the distinction between those who have lost family members or friends and those who have lost a spouse. "I'm sorry, but it's just a very different thing," she pointed out. "When you lose a husband or wife, you've lost your partner—your soul mate. When someone in my world suffers a loss, it stirs up all of my own pain. I start to think, *If Ril were here, I wouldn't be so sad.* So, not only have I lost my partner, but I've also lost the person who could have helped me through *other* hard stuff. The truth is, I have started to think about what it would be like to fill that hole. Maybe that's part of the next phase of things—I don't know."

At the point when we talked, Rosalyn was missing the presence of someone who valued her as an adult, as a woman. But she was also missing Ril and was still focused on keeping his legacy alive for herself and their daughters. This is a balancing act faced by many of the widows with whom I spoke. "Those two little sets of eyes are always watching me," she said. "Matilyn, who's ten now, has started asking about boys. Apparently, there is a little boy in her class who told her he has a crush on her! So, as I move toward the idea of dating and bringing some other man into their lives, I think about the impact of it. The older they get, the more important it is to model good relationship behavior for them, as well as everything else. I mean, I kind of hope they grow up and want to get married and have families of their own, so I want them to see what a beautiful thing that can be.

"Listen," she said as we were wrapping up our conversation, "death happens. It happened to us—and it sucked. But I try really hard not to sulk or feel negative all the time. I have to think positive for all our sakes—mine, the kids', and even Ril's. I guess if you want me to define my process, that would be it: to get stronger and more positive and move forward for the sake of the family."

When we met for the final time, I was struck by how far Rosalyn had traveled in the time since Ril's death. She still has trouble making concrete plans for her life, but she powers through the guilt of moving on alone as best she can. "Arlene, there's a dichotomy between what's in my head and what's in my heart, and maybe there always will be," she said with a sigh. "I try to listen to both but go where my head tells me to! Ril would be devastated if I didn't."

We sat quietly for a few minutes, and I could tell that Rosalyn was trying to wrap her head around the journey she was on. "You know," she said, "there was a point when Ril was ready to let go. He hated being sick and hated what it was doing to me. Knowing how important it was to him that I move on after his death . . . that's what's urging me forward more than anything. We couldn't fulfill our dreams together, so I have to reach for as many of them as I can. For the both of us.

"Maybe it sounds grandiose, but one thing we both wanted to do was change the world in some way—make it a better place by helping others. I guess I'm supposed to try to do that on my own now. I'm not sure exactly how it will happen, but I'm working my way toward it."

Rosalyn left me with an image I find memorable. Small things can loom large in the process of moving forward, and this was one of them. "I bought new sheets," she told me, "and while I was putting them on the bed, I stopped for a second and thought, *I like my bed*. It was a tiny moment, but it felt like a turning point. I realized that a place where I'd once been happy and then been very, very sad was starting to make me happy again. If I can love my pillows, maybe I can learn to love my life."

DONNA

On a trip to California for work, I had an opportunity to visit my friend Constance, who lives in Benicia, California, across the bay from San Francisco. Constance had loved Howard, and we toast to him each time I visit. This trip, she asked me to join her at her Friday-evening pizza-and-wine group, an experience I'd enjoyed on previous visits.

At the end of the evening, a woman named Donna approached me and said she'd be happy to be interviewed for the book. I was delighted to add her to my roster, particularly since she was just my second octogenarian. I knew she'd have a lot to offer me and my readers.

At our first meeting, Donna told me the basics of her story. She'd been married and divorced when she met Ray, to whom she was married for more than twenty-five years when he died at age seventy-three. She had two sons, Steve and Scott, both still living in California. Although she'd once been a dental assistant, she and Ray had made their living buying and selling antiques, and she remains involved in the Benicia Historical Society and Museum. She has also volunteered, cleaning up and restoring the local cemetery's headstones.

After Ray developed dementia, she would wake up at 2:00 a.m. to check on him and find him on the deck, a very dangerous place to be when you live on a hillside. It was time to move him to a convalescent home, as difficult as that was. For the five months he stayed there, she visited every day from noon to 4:30—the period when he was most alert. As she put it, she lost him well before he died, although he did return home for a short time after his stay in the convalescent home.

"After he died," she told me, "I really didn't make many changes. All of my Benicia friends were there for me. But I did have to become independent after decades of having a partner. I had to take over paying the bills and all the other things Ray had done. I honestly wasn't very good at those things. Luckily, one of my sons was patient with me, and I learned.

"The house was fairly easy to take care of. The bigger challenge was overcoming the loneliness. Ray and I had done everything together, and now the house was so quiet! I actually started leaving the TV or radio on just for some noise. The thing that got me through it all was the incredible support of my local community."

When I asked her about doing things on her own, Donna admitted that she still had not been out to dinner or a movie by herself. "I just don't want to do those kinds of things alone," she said. "Luckily, I do have people to go out with when I feel like it."

For Donna, the hardest thing about being suddenly single was the responsibility of making big decisions on her own. And when you own a house, there are a lot of decisions to make! Even so, she's not sorry she decided to stay where she was. "My kids tease me about doing things the old-fashioned way," she laughed. "For example, I still go to the bank teller to get cash instead of taking it out of the ATM. I guess I'm slow that way, but I'll get there."

When I asked Donna about her "process," the response she gave sounded familiar. "I don't think I have one," she said. "I just keep trying to move forward in whatever ways are called for, and keep trying to join in on social occasions even though I miss Ray. For a while, I worked with the Historical Society and did other volunteering, and, of course, I still have to put the effort in to get household things done.

"I know I said that loneliness was the hardest part—but it does get easier. Things like the Friday-night pizza-and-wine group really help, along with similar events in our community."

As had become my habit, I focused my second conversation with Donna on support systems. We'd already established the importance of the Benicia community, and she went into greater detail about it. "Honestly," she said, "I cannot imagine any other place as supportive. When I was first invited to join the pizza-and-wine group—shortly after Ray died—it was made up exclusively of single women. It's come to include some married women as well, but I'd say we all understand one another. When we get together, we don't really talk about our problems. It's more of a chance to get away from them. We started out meeting in a restaurant on the waterfront, but at some point, the owner of the Union Hotel offered us a place to meet—even though we really don't eat or drink that much! I think he saw a need and cared more about us than about money. That's what I mean about a supportive community."

Donna's two married sons have both been helpful in spite of their very busy lives, and this gives her a lot of comfort. "I'm lucky that Steve lives nearby and is always willing to come right over if I call, taking me wherever I need to go," she told me. "But I try not to need him too often, as Steve tries to never disappoint me. I must say, I've been enjoying my sons, including my trips down to Sacramento to see Scott and his wife, Meg. Last time, we spent some time in Old Sacramento, which I remember as a sleepy little town, but it has really developed. And we saw a play, which I enjoyed as well.

"And aside from Steve and Scott, there are people in the neighborhood who would be happy to help. This is a small town, and everyone knows everyone. On top of that, Ray knew a lot of different tradespeople, so I know who to call when I need a professional—and they would never take advantage of me."

I eased the conversation onto the subject of preparations. Had she and Ray done any long-term planning before he got ill? That question got a resounding *yes.* "Although he died in 2008, at the age of seventy-three, Ray and I started planning for our future when we were in our forties, shortly after we got married," she told me. "We even took out a long-term care insurance policy, which ended up being a good thing. We also had a very good financial advisor, who helped us throughout our marriage and has continued helping me afterward for the past twelve years."

In our third conversation, I wanted to discuss a topic specific to Donna: aging alone. She admitted immediately that being a widow in her eighties was fraught with unforeseen challenges. "Naturally, there are health and medical things," she said. "I've had a lot of issues with my vision. And related to that are the new requirements out here that a driver's license has to be renewed every four years. They make you take a pretty involved test to make sure you're still up to it. That has caused me a fair amount of worry, because in California, if you can't drive, you really lose your independence. I'd have no life without a car! There are lots of nice places to walk around where I live, but it's hilly here, so I really can't walk into town anymore; if I want to take a nice walk, I drive to the center of town, park, and then walk.

"If it ever really comes to it, there are some options for senior living about twenty miles away—not that I'm looking forward to that. But I know I shouldn't wait until I really start to fail or until I don't have enough money to do all of the major work the house is going to need."

Donna was quiet for a few moments, and then she said, "You know, that decade between seventy and eighty creeps up on you, then before you know it, it's over. And then things really start to fall apart. I think I just have to stay on top of everything—the house, my health, my ability to move around—and make sure I don't end up isolated and in trouble. That facility I mentioned is for people fifty-five and older and has a lot of amenities. I'd also be closer to my doctors and the best hospitals. I wonder, though . . . right now, the house and yard keep me so busy . . . the cooking and shopping too. I wonder if I'd get bored in a place where everything was provided for me."

In our final meeting, Donna and I continued to discuss the future. Once again, she emphasized her dilemma concerning her living situation. "The future is just so uncertain at this age," she said. "I passed my driver's license test, so for now, that's taken care of. But I've stopped driving at night because of my vision—and who knows what else might go wrong? When you ask about *moving forward*, I wonder what that means for somebody my age. I try not to panic about anything—just prepare.

"I'd really love to stay in my big, roomy house rather than move somewhere cramped and have to get rid of most of my things. But it gets harder each year: taking care of the yard, even going up and down the stairs, which are long and very steep. Physically, the house isn't well laid out for an older person; I learned that when Ray was too sick to come downstairs. But he had me, and I won't have a partner when the time comes. That's the reality, so I know I'll have to make a change at some point. I just hope I know when to do it."

As we wrapped up, Donna counted her blessings. "I guess I went on and on about how hard it will be to leave my house," she said, "but I know how lucky I am. I know many people don't have the options I have. Right now, I can stay where I am, and when the time comes that I need a different arrangement, I can move. I am just trying to keep an open mind. The worst thing in the world is to dig your heels in and refuse to change. You talk about moving forward; I guess to me, that's what it means: making changes when they become the right thing to do."

MARGARET

On another visit to California, a friend and colleague talked to me about her lifelong friend Margaret, who had had learned to move forward along her own path after being widowed at age fifty-nine. I was intrigued by Margaret, partly because she has always lived in the Midwest, in the Twin Cities of Minnesota, and I'd not talked to anyone from that region.

Margaret was married to Mike for thirty-three years. Within five years of his death, she lost her mother, sister, and father—a devastating progression that might have left her paralyzed with grief for a long time. The fact that she wanted to talk to me for this book reflects the strong stuff that Margaret is made of. "I believe helping other widows move forward is such a worthwhile thing," she told me. "I've read a lot of books designed for widows, but most of them focus on grieving. It seems like you are doing something different—something a bit more positive than telling women how to fall apart properly. Honestly, maybe if women hear my story, they'll figure out that if I could experience this much loss and continue to move forward, they can too!

"We were living in a four-bedroom house we'd bought after we started our family. Once Mike knew he was ill, I guess he started thinking about me all alone in that big house. He started suggesting we take these car rides, and he'd point out town houses that he thought were quite nice. I didn't get the point at the time, but later I realized he was giving me permission to move out of our house when he was gone. Suggesting it, really.

"Around that same time, when his health was going downhill pretty fast, I found myself getting depressed. Mike and I had lost a baby girl, Christine, before we had our two children, Marissa and John Michael, who were twenty-seven and twenty-four when Mike died. They are now forty and thirty-eight. I guess the possibility of losing Mike sent me into the deep end. I decided to see a therapist, and she gave me a great piece of advice: 'When you lose a spouse, you shouldn't make any big changes for a year.' This really resonated, and I ended up taking it to heart. I waited a year before thinking about moving, and I thought a lot about my criteria for a new place. I decided I'd have to find something I was really excited about before leaving my family's home. It took me five years, but I did eventually move into a town house. It just made sense, and I found one where I felt I could be happy.

"Mike had also told me he thought I'd remarry, and at the time, I thought he was wrong—but you know what? After five years of dating John, we are committed partners, so I guess Mike knew me pretty well. He knew I'd move forward, even when *I* didn't.

"The thing is, even though women might have more trouble coping with stuff like water heaters, we are definitely better at moving through life on our own. Men tend to need partners—or they *think* they do—while women don't so much need them as decide they want them. At least, that was my case. Interestingly, I ended up choosing someone pretty different from Mike. While my husband was kind of an introvert, John is much more outgoing and social."

Margaret had gone back to school for her master's degree, focusing on family studies and human development. One of the courses that had a profound impact on her was called Women Later in Life. The research she did for it became the basis for her final thesis.

My second meeting with Margaret began with a discussion of support. "I'm lucky to have wonderful friends," she told me. "I know I can call on them whenever I need to. But . . . as generous as they are, it's still hard to go out with couples and not feel like a third wheel." (How well I knew that feeling.) "I'm better off one-on-one, I guess. Being around a happy couple can really stir up my grief over what I've lost."

She returned to the topic of support—but this time, the professional kind. "I mentioned before that I started seeing a therapist when Mike was very ill," she said, "but I don't think I told you how that came about. My sister, Mary Jo, was a nurse, and she's the one who urged me to find someone to talk to. In fact, she did more than that: she sent me a check so I couldn't use money as an excuse! I'm really glad she pushed me, because it helped. And I'm glad I started before Mike died, because I don't know whether I'd have had the psychic energy to start that process afterward.

"I also started going to a support group at the Center for Grief & Loss in Saint Paul. Some of the other widows were still quite raw, and some were further along. To be honest, I thought it would be more helpful than it was. Maybe I'm not a 'group' person; I tend to think things over before I talk about them, so it was a little hard for me to just jump into the conversation in response to the group leader's questions."

Like several of the other women I spoke with, Margaret has not only elicited support, but also has sometimes provided it. When her next-door neighbor was widowed a few years before we spoke, Margaret stepped up to answer her questions and serve as an example. "I'm cautious about offering my opinion on something unless I'm asked," she told me. "I remember being given unsolicited advice, and it wasn't always helpful. For instance, one person told me never to turn down an invitation—which wasn't what I needed to hear. But, being a few years ahead of my neighbor in the process, I figured I had something to offer her. Sometimes we would just share a cup of coffee and chat about 'normal' things. Each of our journeys as widows is unique, but I think it's helpful to have someone in one's life who has walked the same path.

"As Mike's illness progressed, I could no longer sleep in the same bed with him, then in the same room. I'd just lie in bed alone, with Mike in the next room, and cry. I knew that my own life would continue, and, in a way, I was crying over that as well."

Our next meeting was focused on the recent wedding of Margaret's son, John Michael. I was curious about how that had gone, and what she'd learned from the experience.

"Well, first of all," said Margaret, "it was exhausting. There were three different hotels involved, a lot of travel, and a crowd of more than one hundred people from all over the place. I loved seeing my son's friends from high school and college, now all grown up and starting their own lives. As hard as it was to go through such a major family milestone without Mike, it was fulfilling too. At the end of the ceremony, Marissa told her brother how proud their father would have been of him, and we all cried. I've thought back to that moment so often since."

Margaret very much wanted me to know that she doesn't see grief as a linear thing. "Memories and sadness come flooding in for a while; then they recede; then they come back. You really never know when a wave of grief is going to hit you," she said. I nodded in recognition. "I tried to explain this to my daughter, and that milestones, like weddings, can really invite the sadness in."

One thing Margaret is involved in right now is helping a friend, Chris, who is struggling with liver cancer. "I'm working with Chris's daughter to create a CaringBridge website," she told me, "where Chris's friends and family members can check in and find out what's going on with her, read updates from us, and leave messages. It's a really wonderful solution to how to keep people informed and connected without the burden of a million calls and emails. One thing the internet is great for is bringing a community of caring people together in a crisis. We're even putting up photos. I used the site when Mike was ill and figured it would work for Chris's family and friends too."

At the end of our meeting, I shared an experience that had touched me. "I went to a book signing of the author Brad Meltzer," I said, "and although this was for one of his mystery novels, he described his grief for his father when he died as 'a hole in his heart.' At first, he said, he wondered when that hole might heal. But as time went by, he realized that wasn't the point. His father had been an extraordinary man, so of course he'd created a hole. And that hole didn't have to heal; it belonged there. I knew exactly what he meant. We all have our 'holes,' and they mark us as members of a club that no one would want to join. They are part of who we are."

My final talk with Margaret was to be about the future. How did she intend to continue moving forward? Her first response was to say that at some moments, she still doesn't feel as if she *is* moving forward—though most of the time she knows she is. "There has just been so much loss in the intervening years," she noted, "and so many details to take care of after each of my loved ones passed. But . . . I guess I just keep putting one foot in front of the other and keep trying not to be bitter or think, *Why me?* Life's a journey, and whether we like it or not, we're on it until we die."

Margaret had been so generous with me, sharing her thoughts and feelings and memories, that it was surprising when she said that she no longer thinks about these things as often. "Arlene," she said, "don't take this the wrong way, because I have enjoyed our talks, but sitting with you and answering your questions has brought up a lot of memories and feelings that have faded. Sometimes I feel I'm in another place completely now—living another life. I guess in some ways I am, with John.

"Something I read in graduate school after Mike died really resonated with me. The idea of it was that late in their lives, women develop new strengths and enjoy greater freedom. We've gotten over so many hurdles and accomplished so much that we actually feel freer. I think that's true of me."

Margaret now expends a lot of her energy volunteering. She creates videos for her church and for other groups, and some of these have been circulated widely. I sensed her genuine pride when she talked about these accomplishments, as well as her commitment to continuing to develop new skills and do new things. Clearly, this is at the heart of her effort to move forward.

Not surprisingly, Margaret is quick to seize an opportunity to help other widows. Most recently, she has been facilitating Zoom meetings for bereaved women and helping them hold virtual funerals when COVID-19 restrictions keep them from gathering in person. Margaret's journey and her spirit have inspired me greatly, and I told her so as we parted. I thanked her for offering her story to readers of this book, who I hope will find the strength in it inspiring as well.

BARBARA

One afternoon, my friend April called to share the sad news that her good friend Barbara had lost her husband. This was Barbara's second marriage; her first husband had died along with their son in a plane crash twenty years earlier. Widowed twice, the second time after more than twenty years of marriage . . . I just couldn't imagine such a thing.

April wondered if I might be interested in speaking with Barbara, and, of course, I welcomed her unusual perspective. When we first spoke, her second husband, Butch, had been gone for a year and a half.

Right from the start, Barbara was quite candid about her first loss versus her second. "I can only tell you about my own experience," she cautioned. "I wouldn't want anyone to generalize about it. But when I lost my first husband, Ed, and my son, Israel Avi, in that crash, it was devastating in a way that nothing else could ever be. "Two friends stayed with me, along with my mother, and I began seeing a psychologist almost immediately—one who had lost a child herself. She was so helpful. For example, I told her at one point that I kept waking up in the middle of the night, scared to death. She knew that I was a very visual person, so she suggested that when that happens, I visualize wrapping those scary thoughts and dreams in a green plastic bag and sending that package to God. Believe it or not, this advice, along with some breathing exercises she recommended, helped me a lot."

Barbara explained some of the specific differences between her two losses, and they had everything to do with the differences in the relationships themselves. "My first husband was more self-centered," she said. "Maybe that's why I developed a much deeper relationship with Butch. In the end, I recognized that Butch was my soul mate. I'm sure that's why I moved toward him so quickly. He and I made each other better people.

"I went back to work after Ed and Israel Avi were killed, as a science teacher. It was at school that I met Butch, who was working there as an architect on a special project. We actually had some friends in common and began to spend a lot of time together. The more we talked and shared experiences, the deeper our friendship grew. I figured out that you can have two loves of your life. Sadly, you can also lose two loves of your life."

Our conversation turned to the subject of work. "Work can keep you very busy and give you a reason to get up in the morning," she told me. "And, of course, work brought me Butch! But after Butch died, I retired. I just felt that at that point, I needed to create a completely new life in order to move forward."

As I did with the other widows, I asked Barbara about how her friendships were affected by her widowhood. "Butch and I lived in the woods of Vermont, in a summer home that we built together," she told me, "and I was the first one of all my friends up there to lose a spouse. I think it was kind of difficult for some of them to deal with. We had been a part of this group of three couples who ate lunch together every week. After Butch died, the five of us tried it once, and then I quietly dropped out. It just felt wrong, especially for the husbands, who had been Butch's friends. However, I also felt the women really did not want me in this group. It wasn't balanced anymore. In fact, most of the couples we had been friendly with vanished from my life.

"A lot of people suggested that I sell the Florida house, and make a really fresh start with all new things. I think most people thought I'd be better off in town instead of out in the boonies—but I told everyone *no*. What would moving into town do? I'd still be lonely—just with more people on the street. I really don't think anyone can tell you how to move on after you lose a spouse; you have to figure it out and be strong enough to follow your own instincts. I've heard about women who leave their homes quickly, before they've thought it through, and then regret it.

They end up even lonelier than they would have been in familiar surroundings."

Barbara is an artist, and she believes that creating paintings and sculptures has helped her process her emotions. Before she left Vermont, she created an enormous wood sculpture for a hospice group she'd been a part of. Another one of her sculptures is of a woman whose heart has two male figures carved out of it, representing those she lost. "Art is my way of expressing anguish without screaming," she said, "and for searching for the beauty in the world. I like to give my pieces to people who I think might get the same emotional relief from them that I did when I made them.

"I'm sure I'm not different from most grieving people, in that I have good days and bad days. I look for different ways to make myself feel better, and some of them work, while some don't. For example, I became a docent at a small local art museum and didn't like it at all—but a quilting group I joined has worked out really well. It's a place to socialize, keep my hands busy, and get a hug or two from friends. I tried two different gardening groups; one worked out, and the other didn't. So I guess you never know. You just have to keep trying things, joining things, and see what fits and makes you feel better. This is a kind of gift you give yourself—staying active, giving something to others; it all makes your days less empty."

The focus of my second conversation with Barbara was, as usual, support systems. Some of the experiences she encountered were unhelpful, while others were extremely helpful. Barbara shared that she learned to move away from the negative ones and toward those that were positive.

"I was really upset when the synagogue I belonged to at the time Ed died wouldn't let me say the traditional mourner's prayer—the Kaddish—because I was a woman, and only men were supposed to say it. My friend Sandy took me to some other synagogues, including a Reconstructionist one that allowed me to say the prayer. I really liked the rabbi there, who seemed very present and supportive. Having moved back to Florida, I no longer belong to a formal religious group but to two interfaith groups, and I believe I am a spiritual person.

"I guess I was actively looking for support wherever I could find it. There was this fabulous counselor from hospice I saw for a while, and a number of religious support groups I joined, but as time went on, those fell apart. Most of the people in them were women, and they all seemed to move away to be near their children.

"One psychologist I saw wasn't helpful in the least; he just wanted to prescribe medication, which I didn't want to take. At one point, he told me that the work we would do together would make me happy again. I looked around his office at the pictures of his beautiful family and said, 'Doctor, if you went home one day and your family was just *gone,* do you think anything—any therapist or counselor—would make you happy?'"

Today, Barbara is busy reorganizing her house and creating a new studio where she can make art. She explained to me that she is careful to build in time to decompress and rest by reading and thinking, or practicing Tai Chi. Clearly, she has become (or has always been) a person eager for new pursuits. She counts Talmud study, photography, and singing in a chorus among her hobbies. "I just try things on," she said. "Some of them are a good fit, and some, I let go of." This reminded me of my various conversations about letting go of negative people—which, Barbara agreed, is just as important.

"People can be positive or negative," she noted, "but my supportive friends have definitely helped me become stronger as well as more independent. For example, there's Robert. He kept telling me I needed to put a cover on my well, but he was having some health problems and wasn't up to helping me with it. That doesn't mean he wasn't supportive. He advised me on what to do—how to use moving pads and insulation—and I did it all myself. That ended up being good for my self-confidence.

"I am also lucky enough to have a great, trustworthy plumber, who, in turn, has recommended a lot of other repair people who have worked out well and haven't taken advantage of me just because I'm a woman alone. I realize these guys are paid employees and not pals, but I definitely consider them part of my support system."

Looking toward the future, Barbara was philosophical: "I look around and see more and more women of a certain age trying to figure out how they might survive without going into assisted living. It's something I wonder about too. Will it be possible to figure out an alternative that involves a community instead of an institution? It's something we've all started to talk about."

The next time I met with Barbara, she started by telling me about her having to leave her house for two days due to loss of electricity from a severe windstorm. A friend was kind enough to put her up. "The thing is," she said, laughing, "I have a generator—but I don't know how to use it! Butch never explained the thing, and I never asked. Now, I know I have to figure it out. It probably isn't that hard, but I couldn't exactly do it with the lights out, so I have to prepare now for the next disaster."

Changing the subject, she mentioned that she really likes serving as a role model for others. For example, she makes beaded necklaces, and when she wears them out, other women tend to admire them. "Some friends said they wanted to learn to make them too," she explained, "and suddenly my friends are beaders. They're even converting rooms in their houses into craft rooms. It makes me happy because I think we can all be artists. Making things is therapeutic, whatever your situation. I think Butch would love that I'm being emulated in this way.

"Another thing I've done is start a Green Team at my synagogue—a group concerned with conservation and sustainability. We meet with groups from other religious organizations, including a Baptist Church that calls its group Go Green for God. It has become really important to me to expend energy helping others.

"In my bereavement book group, we discuss our particular bumps along the road. For example, some people still have trouble sleeping; others find they can't listen to music. A lot of the women have nightmares, including me. With help from this group, I've learned to sit up in bed and say, 'Everything is all right'—out loud, as if someone could hear me. I say other things out loud too—reminders, such as 'Turn off the oven' or 'Lock the door behind you.' There's nothing wrong with talking, even if you are the only one there!"

Barbara is very aware of small acts of kindness and noted that they can be more meaningful than people realize. "A small gesture can have a big effect," she explained. "For instance, last Friday night was soup night at the synagogue. "The people I was going to sit with were late, so I just took my soup and sat down at an empty table. A few minutes later, a young woman I didn't really know left her group and came to sit with me. We chatted until my friends came, and after I introduced them all, the woman went back to her friends. I thought that was very thoughtful . . . that she saw someone who might be in need of companionship and did something about it.

"In general, I think I'm doing quite well in my process of grieving and healing. Other people have told me as much, anyway—including a psychologist and a neuropsychologist who specializes in grief. They're both social acquaintances of mine, but I trust their judgment. The other reason I think I'm doing well is that I have observed others who aren't. Maybe I'm lucky that I've been through widowhood before—although *lucky* is a strange word to use. The difference is that the first time, I was working and had a supportive work environment. I was surrounded by people, whether I wanted to be or not. This time, I have to make the effort to be with people and socialize. That isn't to say I'm never alone. I like my alone time—who doesn't?—but I recognize the need I have to go out, do things, see people, so I work at it.

"In fact, I make a point of getting out of the house at least once a day—to a café, to walk the dog, to run an errand. My psychologist friend confirmed that this is important, that people who isolate themselves at home day after day have a much harder time moving forward. My various activities help, of course. Wednesday night is chorus. Friday evening is synagogue. And there are the less frequent things too, like the monthly meeting of the digital camera society I belong to. The meetings of the bereavement book group are always scheduled for weekends because we all share in the fact that our married friends want to be with their spouses then."

In our next meeting, Barbara told me about an interesting experience she had about a year and a half after her son and first husband died. She called it an "*aha* moment." She was driving along a busy road when a truck hit a car in front of her. The car's bumper came loose and flew toward Barbara's windshield. "At that moment," she said, "I realized that I could just do nothing and die or turn the wheel and live. I turned the wheel. When it was all over and I thought about it, I realized, *Oh, I guess I do want to live.*

"Nothing that dramatic happened after Butch died, but, of course, I had to make the decision to live yet again. Every day was a struggle for a while, naturally. I put off selling our little Vermont house for a year because I just . . . couldn't do it. We'd physically built that house together. Of course, that was exactly why I needed to sell it, among other reasons. But I needed that year to become whole on my own—you know?"

I did know.

"I have to admit, I'm tired of making myself over. My friends think I'm amazing because I'm so busy, so involved in things, a *role model*. Which is all great, but it does get tiring. I think what they may not realize is that I don't exactly have a choice. I mean, what are my options? I can either make myself over by getting busy with things, or I can just sit and rot in a corner. And that's just not *me*.

"Just this past weekend, I woke up—the mornings are hardest for me—and I recognized that I needed to be with people. So I called up some friends who like to do crafty things, and we went off to a bunch of yard sales to find supplies. These are the kinds of people I need in my life, people who share my passions and hobbies. Whoever you are, you have to find like-minded souls and bring them into your world. They're out there; I promise! It's all about building a life again."

ANUSUYA

My next widow, Anusuya ("Anu"), brings great depth to the journey of widowhood. A friend of mine of twenty-seven years, who knew both Howard and me and was aware of this book and my desire to be supportive of other widows, talked to me about her cousin, a widow, in India. She introduced me via email to Anusuya and recommended I interview her.

Anusuya's husband, Gautam, died in early 2016, at the age of fifty-eight. He'd suffered from Huntington's disease, a degenerative illness for which there is no cure, but his death came swiftly in his sleep from a pulmonary embolism. "I suppose you could say I was both prepared and not prepared," remarked Anusuya. "My mother-in-law, Manjulika, was living with us at the time, which was helpful, but we were both grieving—she for a son, and I for a husband. Our two children, Arjun and Megha, were supportive, of course, but they had their own busy lives to take care of."

Anusuya has chosen to remain in her house—her home. She really didn't even consider moving, partly because of her mother-in-law, who was eighty at the time and the rock of the family. "She was the image of strength the rest of us emulated," said Anu.

In the months after Gautam's death, Anusuya busied herself with the necessary paperwork and business. Then she returned to her usual routine. "I never crashed," she said. "When I felt sad, I hid it and maintained a strong exterior for the sake of my family. Of course, when I was alone, I let my feelings of grief come out—but never in front of others. We even had a cake on Gautam's birthday."

When I asked her how it felt to lose a spouse so suddenly, she told me she was grateful for it, for his sake. "He got to go quickly and with dignity," she said, "rather than gradually losing control of all of his functions and dying bedridden, which is how it could have happened." Nearly every widow I spoke with used the word *grateful* at some point, though perhaps not in this context. "I find it's so important to remember the happiness and not dwell on the sorrow," Anusuya said. "I can't just sit around and focus on death. When we get together as a family now, we talk about all the good things we remember about Gautam. We invoke his presence without negativity. That's the only way we can move forward.

"Of course, there are moments when I can't help it; the emptiness comes through, and I want to just be a social recluse." This led directly into a conversation about socializing, and Anu's feelings on the subject mirrored those of others. "Too much going out makes me feel like an outsider," she commented. "I can be at a party and suddenly feel like I'm going to fall apart." When I confessed that I hadn't attended a wedding or party in over six years, she replied, "The thing is, I used to be such a gregarious person—a party person. I think my personality has changed! My daughter, Megha, tries to get me to go out, telling me I'll have a good time once I'm there, but most of the time, I just can't face it. She thinks I'm just being stubborn, but she simply doesn't understand, the way another widow might.

"When my brother-in-law's daughter got married, I attended and really wanted to participate in some of the rituals—the small customs—but I just couldn't handle it. I had to leave. A year later, my brother-in-law told me that it had hurt him. I felt terrible about it, but I couldn't explain my actions in a way he could understand. I just kept saying that I couldn't do it.

"Maybe this makes it sound as if I'm not moving forward, but really, I *am*. That's my only option, because if you don't move forward, you can go into a downward spiral. I've talked about this with a few friends who were widowed around the same time I was.

One of them had always been seen as a strong woman, a tower of strength. People thought she breathed fire, so I guess they weren't that worried about her when she lost her husband. But the truth is, she just collapsed. She became a shadow of herself. To this day—five years later—she struggles through every minute. It's impossible to predict how we'll react to such an event. I just know that for me, I have to do what I can to keep going each day, but allow myself to avoid things I can't handle."

Hear! Hear!

When I spoke with Anusuya to discuss her support system, she immediately praised her children; her mother, Mamata; and her mother-in-law, Manjulika: "They really helped me process and deal with the anger and frustration I felt—and there was a lot of it. As time passed, it did get easier to grieve in private, but at first, I had to let my feelings out sometimes, and I know this hurt my family. Soon, I began to try to lead as normal a life as possible—in part, to protect them and keep them from being worried about me. The result was that I did feel more normal, so I guess it was good for all of us."

Anu talked about her friends as well. "I have wonderful friends," she told me, "and they really gathered around me when I needed them. They were especially helpful after my son's wedding, when all of that activity was over and I finally had time to mourn."

I asked her more about the wedding, honestly dumbfounded by the idea of having to celebrate such a joyous occasion so soon after the death of a spouse. "Arjun actually carried a large portrait of his father around," she told me. "It was just so important to him that his father be present for the occasion. He understood that his father's physical presence was an impossibility, but he really believed he was with us in spirit. So did I. I think that's why I was able to walk my son down the aisle; I felt Gautam's presence there with us. And when I needed some extra strength, I thought about something my mother-in-law said: 'You have to do more for the living than the dead.'

"Gautam remains with us to this day. There is rarely a conversation in which his name doesn't come up. We all feel his absence, so we talk about what he might say, what he might do. We even make jokes about him. None of us wants to be 'over' him; we feel his absence, but we invite his presence always."

When I asked Anusuya about learning to live independently, she pointed out that she had been moving in that direction well before Gautam's death. "The disease he had causes a slow decline, and we'd been feeling this for quite a while," she explained. "I'd already begun taking over many of the tasks that used to fall to him. I'd already become the cosigner on certain documents and had already accepted help from friends who knew that Gautam was growing less capable. As he became more stressed and depressed, I simply took over what I could. My son, Arjun, was helpful when it came to sorting out our money situation. It was also a benefit that Gautam had worked at a bank, so his colleagues were there for me as well."

Anu told me that she has become a go-to person when people around her lose their spouses. "They want all kinds of advice and information from me," she said. "How many death certificates to order, things like that. A lot of times, I have to tell them I just don't remember the answers. There are really big blanks in my memory of the weeks following Gautam's death."

I told her I thought that was understandable—and that she wasn't alone in it. And when I considered how suddenly her husband had passed, and how soon her son's wedding had followed, I thought it was kind of a miracle that she retained any recollection of that time at all!

I asked Anusuya what she did to take care of herself—to be her own support system—after Gautam died. She immediately mentioned the importance of her trip to Munnar, in the hills of India, with her mother and mother-in-law: "Initially, I agreed to the trip for the sake of my mother-in-law, Manjulika, but it was just as beneficial to me and my mother, Mamata, as it was to her.

"Now, every anniversary of Gautam's death is remembered with flowers and candles. We make an occasion of it by cooking silly little things he liked. My son, Arjun, and my daughter-in-law, Madhurima, live in London now, so we video chat with them. Maybe this year, I'll even go visit. I love London because I feel independent there, just wandering and visiting museums while the children are at work."

In general, Anusuya feels she is doing quite well at this point. "I have spent a lot of time being a rock for my family, but now I think maybe I can actually be happy," she told me. "It's been important to realize that at the end of his life, Gautam suffered a lot of pain, but so did I. Just watching him fall apart was the source of pain for me—and all that pain is gone now. His pain and mine. I don't really cry much anymore. It's kind of amazing. I guess the sadness now has to do with the fact that he can't see how well I'm doing at moving forward."

As soon as Anu and I sat down together for our next chat, she told me that both her mother, Mamata, and mother-in-law, Manjulika, had died. Now both of the supportive moms who'd helped her so much were gone, and she was completely alone in the house. I expressed my deep sympathy, remembering my own reckoning with solitude.

"My mother's passing was peaceful," she told me. "She was having trouble breathing, and I thought we'd better go to the hospital. I was walking her to the car, and she collapsed—right there, in the driveway—and died instantly. You know, my mother hated hospitals, so again, perhaps this quick death was a blessing. She's moved on, and now I have to as well."

I wasn't really sure what to ask this woman who had borne so much loss in just a few short years, so I asked about her current habits. Anusuya understood immediately that I was trying to ascertain the small details that indicate a seismic change in one's life. "You know," she said, "even cooking and eating have changed completely. Meals don't have the same significance that they did before—with Manjulika, and then with Mamata passing. Now, I just have to prepare food for myself. When I am hungry, I figure out what I want and make it. If I don't feel like eating, I don't bother. There's a loss of structure in the day that meal preparation and eating always provided. I didn't think about it much before, but I think about it now—the liberation of it . . . but also the loss. You know, it's the little things that have the biggest impact."

Anusuya isn't really sure what the future holds at this point. Each day, she weighs her options. "I think about making big plans but also small ones," she says. "I could go live at the beach. My daughter, Megha, lives in Goa, and she'd love it if I moved there. But I wonder whether doing that would mean I was living my daughter's life and not my own. For now, I guess I'm in limbo.

"One thing I know for sure is that I am tired of mourning. I wouldn't say that I'm unhappy, and I wouldn't call myself lonely. Lots of people have offered to come and stay with me. It is a tradition among Indian people to prop up others, to offer to be present. I have to tell them that I just don't feel I need that right now.

"Honestly, I feel that starting fresh is the best thing I can do right now. I guess you could say I am a spiritual person; I definitely believe that everything happens for a reason, and that life is a series of challenges we are expected to meet. For fifteen years, my challenge was to be the best caregiver I could be. Now, that part of my journey is complete, and I have to meet new challenges. At this point, instead of taking care of others, I must learn to take care of myself. There may be a further purpose for me, but I am still waiting for it to appear. I hope I am up to fulfilling it."

As the world was facing a widespread lockdown in response to the COVID-19 pandemic, Anu and I had our final conversation. Naturally, we talked about this dire situation. "I think we're all discovering new things about ourselves," she said. "The people I know tend to be older, and they aren't really complaining about not being able to socialize. In fact, they seem to be adjusting well to the 'new normal.' And I guess I am too."

I'd already shared with Anusuya my concept of being *almost* happy, and we talked about it again. "Yes," she said, "contentment is a good place to land when you are widow. It means you've truly realized that a piece of your life is in the past, but you can find balance in this new piece. As for 'moving forward,' I think I will always strive to achieve small goals and learn small lessons throughout the rest of my life. I believe that now, after having shed all of the responsibilities I had for others, *I* am my primary responsibility. I have to grow and learn within that context. Just the other day, I wanted something sweet, so I baked myself a cake! I'd call that progress."

Before we parted, Anu confessed that she still had moments in which she got lost in the land of *what if.* "What if things had been different?" she said. "And not just with Gautam, but also with all the various choices I've made. I do think everyone comes into our lives for a reason, but when they are gone, you can't help wondering why. So, yes, I think back. But I never let these thoughts send me into the past. I just keep moving forward.

"Currently, I am looking into volunteering, using my skills to help kids in underprivileged communities communicate. I'd like to help children who don't necessarily have access to professional help. The thought of this gives me a lot of energy!"

SHARON

I met Sharon quite by chance, while getting my eyeglasses re-paired—and, if you recall my thoughts about eyeglasses from Chapter 1, you'll understand the significance of that. Unlike the other widows I've included in this book, Sharon wasn't introduced to me by anyone; I believe Howard brought us together.

At our first meeting, which we scheduled during her lunch break from work, it became clear to me that Sharon brought unique experiences to the mix. In 1999, Sharon's husband, Dennis, was diagnosed with advanced prostate cancer that had already metastasized. They were told that the hospitals in Jamaica, where they lived, were not equipped to treat him and were advised to go to Miami—which they ultimately did, along with their two young children, Sorenson, six, and Dominique, seven. Sharon placed the children in a local parochial school. They moved in with cousins until a year later, when they found a small house, where Sharon still lives. They purchased the house in anticipation of a time when Dennis would no longer be there for her. She was thirty-two years old at the time, and he was twenty-five years her senior. They also found a doctor—a fellow Jamaican—in whom they placed their confidence.

While undergoing treatment and building up the strength he'd need to undergo surgery, Dennis taught some science courses at the University of Miami and Sylvan Learning Center. As Sharon had previously worked for Dennis's optical business in Jamaica, she located work in that field in Miami. She continues to work for a commercial optical company. Although she found the move from Jamaica to Miami difficult, she knew it was best for her husband. "The whole process was incredibly draining," said Sharon, "but we just took each day and tried to make the best of it. I was happy for Dennis that even with what was basically a terminal diagnosis, he was able to teach. I know that meant a lot to him."

In 2003, when Dennis's condition worsened to the point where he needed both of his legs amputated, the couple felt they had no choice but to send their children to New York to stay with relatives for several weeks. "We both wanted to spare them the pain of watching their father die," Sharon said. "In the end, Dennis couldn't talk, but he could still write. He'd write little notes to me when he had the strength. Eventually, though, the cancer attacked his brain, and there was no more communication. Really, no hope. It was terrible."

I knew that her sharing all of this with me—little more than a stranger—had to be difficult, but she insisted that it was integral to her story, and she wanted to share the details with other widows who might read my book.

"We can continue next time," I told her, and we ended our initial session on that sad note.

When we got together again, Sharon was ready to discuss her continuous process of moving forward. "It began with concern for the well-being of my children, of course," she said. "They were my main concern, in spite of how bad I felt. I had trouble sleeping, trouble eating. The world was bleak, and I could barely get myself to work. I guess you'd call that depression, but all I knew was that I needed help. I consulted a doctor who prescribed Zoloft, which did calm me down—to the point of lethargy! I had to stop taking it if I wanted to function. Ultimately, I realized I didn't need medication; I just needed time and purpose.

"Having to go to work helped me. Maybe other women have told you the same thing, but when you go to work, you have to leave your troubles outside and be productive. I couldn't afford to lose my job, so I just buckled down and did each task in front of me. On top of that, working meant that I was interacting with others apart from my own kids—socializing. I would have been terribly isolated without my colleagues."

Sharon told me that faith played an important role in her process of healing, providing comfort as well as another arena in which to socialize. "It really helped me to talk to people at church—including some who had lost spouses as well," she said. "It was a safe space for me when I needed one. The pastor had provided spiritual guidance for Dennis when he was alive, so I knew he cared about more than just preaching; he cared about us as people. After Dennis passed, he helped me see that my husband was at peace and in a good place, watching over me. This genuinely made me stronger. It made me feel that at some point, we might be together again.

"Over the course of his illness, Dennis and I had many conversations about what would be best for me and the kids after his death. I didn't want to fail him, so I kept thinking about what he'd said he wanted for them: happy lives and a good education. He also wanted me to sell our optical care store as well as our farm, both in Jamaica. We'd even talked about the possibility that someday I might bring a new man into the kids' lives . . . though it would be a while before I could even think about that."

When I asked Sharon what she thought her greatest challenge was, she immediately mentioned finances. "We had run up some credit card debt because of our move and Dennis's medical bills," she explained. "It was on me to get it all sorted out, and I really hadn't had much to do with our finances before. In working with various companies to get the debt on track toward being paid off, I learned all about handling money. I got over my fear of it. If I needed more time on a payment, I'd just call up the company and get an extension. Some of our debts were forgiven after I talked to the companies. Honestly, after all that, I felt like there was no business matter I couldn't handle. What I didn't think about was the fact that we'd gone from two incomes to one. The kids were nine and ten at this point, and I knew I'd never really get out of debt on just my salary; I'd have to make some other changes. I sat down and made a spreadsheet of all our expenses and my income, and also our assets. It turned out that our house was worth a lot more than we'd paid for it, so I refinanced it and used the equity to pay off our remaining debts. Being able to do that really made me feel in charge of my life. Eventually, I even figured out how to put some money away. I think Dennis would be proud of me."

Sharon grew quiet at this point, and I sensed she was thinking back on her marriage.

"Dennis and I had some ups and downs," she said after a short while. "I guess all couples do—especially when there are children. But he was a really good husband and father. He was my first and only real love, and when I think about him, I feel at peace. I think my ability to move forward comes from knowing what a good life we had—even if it did end sooner than we'd wanted it to."

Our next meeting began with a conversation about second relationships. Sharon has been involved with someone for several years now, and it has presented her with challenges. "I care deeply for Greg," she told me, but he does bring a certain kind of negative energy into my life that I don't like. I think the fact that I was married before makes him insecure, like he's competing with Dennis's ghost. That can be draining, and I really don't want to deal with it, so I find myself keeping things from him. For instance, if it's Dennis's birthday or our anniversary, and I'm thinking about him, I just do it in private. I'm honestly not sure that's good for me or for our relationship—but it's how it is. I have no interest in erasing Dennis's memory from my life. What I really want to ask Greg is, 'How would you feel if you were gone and I just forgot about *you?*'

"I don't really know what the future holds, but I know that peace of mind is really important to me at this point. And I don't think that comes from relationships; I think it comes from finding purpose. I am lucky to have my work at an optical company, and I've also gotten involved in politics—which I love. I've worked on several campaigns, and even when I'm not doing that, I have these long philosophical and political discussions with friends and on Facebook. Sharing my thoughts and opinions about what's going on in the world has become really important to me. I can see myself going back to Jamaica at some point and getting involved in politics there."

On a softer note, Sharon expressed her love of gardening. "Back in Jamaica, I was a farmer," she told me. "That gave me a strong foundation in horticulture, and now I grow herbs, vegetables, and other things I can use to make healthy meals. There's something wonderful about putting your hands in the earth; there's nothing else like it. Nothing more *real*. And there's no pleasure like watching something you planted bear fruit. I guess, also, it connects me to Dennis, because it's something we used to do together. When I'm in my garden, I feel close to him. He's still with me in those moments, and we're still married."

Sharon and I were meeting for one final time, and I wanted to talk about the future. "I'm definitely moving forward, even as we speak," she declared. "Unfortunately, I have to focus on my own health right now though." She explained that she had fibroids the doctors were monitoring, but so far, there was no need for surgery. "Once I feel healthy again," she said, "I'll be able to focus on really being happy—maybe for the first time since Dennis died. I've decided my happiness depends on three things: gardening, politics, and basketball—watching it, not playing it. Maybe these seem like trivial things, but they keep me balanced and on the path forward to a happy future."

In previous conversations, Sharon had discussed the possibility that she and her children might return to Jamaica. Over time, she changed her mind about that. "I will always love my home country," she said, "but it really doesn't make sense for us to move back there—I know that in my heart. There's just too much crime and poverty and not enough opportunities for Sorenson and Dominique. At one time, Dominique had goals in the medical field, planning to take such skills back to Jamaica. But as she continues her academic studies, she intends to stay in the States. Sorenson is happy here as well. It has been sixteen years since Dennis died, and Dominique is now studying to be a physician, and Sorenson works in sales."

Sharon told me she's proud of all that she accomplished in guiding young children into adulthood, both educationally and emotionally. Sorenson is now twenty-six, and Dominique is twenty-eight.

"Today, my goals include traveling around the States and internationally—something I haven't ever had the time or money to do," she said. "I'd love to see France and Sweden, especially Stockholm, where a lot of Dennis's friends live. In fact, we named Sorenson after one of them. My sister lives in Canada, and I'd love to spend some time with her. The thing about traveling is that it's something Dennis and I had always wanted to do together—so now that the kids are grown, I figure I'd better do it for the both of us."

Along with the rest of the widows, Sharon and I agreed that mourning a spouse is a long process—possibly an endless one. "I still continue to adjust to life without Dennis," she said. "He is still present in so many situations, though not all of them. It's sort of like my garden. I have managed to find and cultivate some of the plants I fell in love with back in Kingston, and when I see them, they carry me back to the past. But I also have lots of new plants that have no connection to the past at all; they represent my life now and all of the beauty I foresee in the future."

MANY JOURNEYS

"Water seeks its own level." For Howard and me, that was true—on the surface, anyway. We were from the same city, went to the same college, came from similar backgrounds, and were both goal-oriented. It didn't hurt that we liked the same foods as well. Below the surface, however, we absolutely were not the same. It did not take long for us to discover this, and we spent a lifetime working through those differences.

You could say that the above maxim about water applies to me and the various widows I've interviewed for this book. We certainly have something significant in common. But beyond the fact that we've lost our life partners lie many differences—in background, philosophy, sexual orientation, you name it. On top of that, we were widowed at a variety of ages and have been grappling with the experience for various lengths of time. So which is more important: our differences or the particulars that have emerged as being universal to widowhood?

Today, I would say they are *equally* important.

When I set out to add other stories to my own, I didn't have a clear idea of what would result from that process. I certainly didn't anticipate the close and enduring bond I'd form with women I barely knew or didn't know at all. I just knew that one experience of widowhood—my own—probably wouldn't tell a full enough story to enlighten all those just embarking on the path or anticipating (probably dreading) what it might feel like. I hoped my readers would be diverse in their circumstances, so ultimately, I endeavored to tell enough stories that each person who reads *Moving Forward* might find a situation they can relate to. I hope I've done that.

While widowhood isn't one experience, there are many things about it that do seem constant. I have shared with you many of the fears, concerns, problems, logistics, and situations I have faced along my own path, and have gone on to interview others about those same matters. Should I stay in my marital house? Will I ever feel like seeking out a new partner? Why don't people understand that I don't want to join the party—and maybe I never will? Although the answers to these questions are as unique as the women I spoke with, I've discovered that we in the "widow's club" feel the same way about a lot of things—and that in itself is extremely comforting. I'm not alone in my experience. I'm not the first to feel these feelings. And neither are you.

If there's a theme running through this book, it is that of moving forward—hour by hour, day by day, year by year. My journey is one illustration of how this might look, and each of the other women here has painted her own picture, sharing her own processes, time frames, mistakes, triumphs, and wisdom.

It has taken me a long time to gain the perspective necessary to write *Moving Forward*, but that has been part of my journey too. I am so much stronger and more capable now than I was a few years ago. The view ahead has grown so much clearer, while looking back has become easier and less fraught with grief. I've gained valuable skills, made new connections, and begun defining my life as it *is*, rather than as it *was*. Perhaps it seems presumptuous, but I believe you can do all of this too, sooner or—as in my case—later. Widowhood is many things, but it is not a process that ends. It's life, and life is an open-ended journey! I thank you for sharing a bit of my journey with me, and I wish you well along your own.

—Arlene Sacks

About three weeks before Howard died, he turned to me, using his elbow to prop himself up and put his hand under his chin. "Please do not forget me," he said. I looked at him and replied in my usual humorous and loving way, "Are you insane? That could never happen."

Now, no one who reads this book will forget him either.

CONTINUED AUTHOR BIO

Previously, Arlene Sacks has served as dean of the PhD, EdD, and MA programs at Union Institute & University and she has directed graduate programs at Barry University and St. Thomas University, both in Miami, Florida. She earned her doctorate at West Virginia University.

Arlene is the author of three editions of *Special Education: A Reference Book for Policy and Curriculum Development.* Other notable publications to which she has contributed include *The Developmental Process of Positive Attitudes and Mutual Respect: A Multicultural Approach to Advocating School Safety, The Full Service School: A Holistic Approach to Serving Children in Poverty,* and "Positive Peace Education: From Philosophy to Curriculum."